Inviting Volunteers to Minister

John Cionca

Inviting Volunteers to Minister

Stories and Strategies from Seven Effective Churches

STANDARD
PUBLISHING
Cincinnati, Ohio

Inviting Volunteers to Minister

Cover and inside design, Liz Howe
Editor, Lynn Perrigo
Acquisitions editor, Ruth Frederick

Published by The Standard Publishing Company, Cincinnati, Ohio
A division of Standex International Corporation
Printed in the United States of America

06 05 04 03 02 01 00 99   5 4 3 2 1

ISBN 0-7847-0947-5

Dedication

To Barbara

Who touches the lives of children
through the ministry team she loves and serves
at Calvary Church

Acknowledgments

+ + + + + + +

The staffing and training of volunteers is the primary task of an educational specialist. Ministers who do an effective job in this endeavor spend an incredible amount of time developing their ministry teams. For this reason, I cannot express deep enough appreciation to the education pastors of the seven churches that made this resource possible. They have freely shared their time and insights. And while other churches have marketed and sold their materials, these colleagues have given us permission to use and adapt them as needed. So a heartfelt thanks goes out to Mark Clark, King Chapman, Norm Cruikshank, Hal Edmonds, Will Gatling, Jay Hostetler, Walt Pitman, and Larry Mills. You are teammates and friends.

Appreciation is also due to the support team that transformed the interviews, notes, and drafts into the finished product that you now hold in your hand. So thanks to Roger and Andrea Palms for your editorial teamwork, and to Gloria Metz, Joan Christenson, and Amy Teske for your word-processing teamwork.

And saving the best for last, we again say, *"Thanks be to God who gives us the victory through our Lord Jesus Christ!"*

Table of Contents

+ + + + + + +

Preface

✚ ✚ ✚ ✚ ✚ ✚ ✚

For the past fifteen years, I have been surveying congregations as to their most challenging Christian education problems. Without even a close runner-up, the greatest need is always the recruitment and retention of volunteers. Finding enough volunteers to run an effective educational ministry is a challenge to both small and large congregations; to church plants and centenarians; to urban, suburban, and rural parishes; and to congregations of evangelical, mainline, and charismatic affiliation. Obviously, if there are some staffing secrets out there, most of us are eager to discover them.

Before tackling this resource, I also asked hundreds of pastors to tell me about what is working well in their educational programs. These ideas led to a few dozen interviews, which eventually led to the seven chapters you have before you. What you have in *Inviting Volunteers to Minister* is an insider's look at how seven effective churches go about staffing their educational programs. I have chosen to highlight the areas where each church has made a special, though perhaps not unique, contribution.

As you read these stories, you will notice more similarities than differences. What I have learned is that churches that are effective in directing volunteer service are usually doing the same things. They are passionate about their call to impact lives, develop an atmosphere conducive to service, are people-oriented, cultivate prospects, interview and check backgrounds, train their people, and supply plenty of encouragement and appreciation. The beauty of diversity is that each of these churches wraps its own personality and emphases around these leadership practices. Thus, we can both enjoy and learn from the models of ministry shared by these colleagues.

Chapter One

It's Only Natural: An Atmospheric Approach

**Sierra Madre Congregational Church
Sierra Madre, California**

It doesn't take you long at Sierra Madre Congregational Church to realize that service is everybody's business. Ministry within the body of Christ is not reserved for a select few. Rather, it's the expectation of the congregation that the average Christian will get involved in service.

"Every member is a minister" is a saying heard in many congregations, but at Sierra Madre Congregational Church, they really practice it. Perhaps it's because the pastor himself frequently asks the congregation, "What is the motto of our church?" The congregation responds out loud, "At SMCC, every member is a minister." It's not uncommon for him to ask that question a couple of times a month, whether during the message or at some other time in the service.

It is within this environment that Larry Mills, minister of Christian education, oversees a leadership team that invites volunteers to serve. Larry tells us about the ministry at Sierra Madre.

A Pervasive Atmosphere of Service

✠ ✠ ✠ ✠ ✠ ✠ ✠

Our children's minister once commented that she has had the easiest time recruiting people to serve here of any church she has been a part of. I would have to concur. Something has developed that makes recruiting very easy for us at Sierra Madre Congregational Church.

My philosophy of ministry is spelled out in the acrostic, COME: **C**haracter, **O**rganization, **M**essage, and **E**vidence. I want people to *come* to Christ, to *come* into a relationship with the body of Christ, and to *come* forward in response to an invitation to serve (Matthew 4:19). Once they indicate a willingness to serve, it is my responsibility to match them to a ministry opportunity within the *organization*. Once they are in the structure, their job is to teach the unchanging *message* of hope and direction found in the Scriptures. The *evidence* that we are doing something right at Sierra Madre is that people are involved throughout the church. They are doing something for the kingdom in service to the Lord.

I think a healthy atmosphere for service begins with our staff. The collegiality of our staff and the fun that we have together project to the rest of the church body that ministry is fun. There is joy in serving Jesus! The congregation notices our commitment to serve and our appreciation for one another.

Being a part of the body of Christ suggests that a person is not fulfilled until he has a ministry or area of service. Since an atmosphere of service exists at Sierra Madre, we find that people *expect* to be approached about ministry by one of the Christian education staff members. Of course, I have urged our staff not to approach anybody until they have bathed that encounter in prayer. We believe that the Holy Spirit is at work preparing people for the contacts we make.

We do very few public announcements about our needs. There is no general SOS for help. Instead, our pastor freely celebrates the good things that are happening throughout the church by having a "look what God is doing" time during the services, which includes testimonies from teachers and students. Due to this positive atmosphere, most people that we approach about serving usually respond with, "Oh, I have been thinking about that. That is something that I would like to try. Tell me more."

Pushing People Out of the Nest

+ + + + + + +

One of our goals is to push people out of the comfort of their nests. To help us do this, every teacher of an adult class has the responsibility of encouraging his class members to find an area of service. Nobody has priority "rights" to anybody in his class. We have found that when somebody leaves a class to teach or fill another area of service, additional people invariably show up to fill those vacated seats. This is not because we're a huge church. In fact, we meet in a small, crowded facility. But people recognize that good things are happening at Sierra Madre and that's attractive—it draws them in deeper.

We have young people who are beginning to understand that they, too, can be part of ministry. Even fifth and sixth graders have ministry opportunities. Roles for young people beyond participation in the youth choir include being tutors, mentors, nursery assistants, child-care helpers, and teachers' aides. We have a program called TICS: "Teens in Christian Service." We help teens implement what they are learning. Involvement in ministry is the graduation point for them.

Pastoral Support

+ + + + + + +

One advantage I have here at Sierra Madre is that Pastor Richard Anderson is pro-Christian education. He knows how tough the job is. More importantly, he has a tremendous love for the church and believes in involvement and service. Thus, our motto: "At SMCC, every member is a minister." The pastor wants to see people grow beyond being sponges. He sincerely desires their growth through serving in some type of ministry.

Evangelism and discipleship are also much on the pastor's heart. He believes that Sunday school teachers, youth workers, camp counselors, VBS workers, and all of the Christian education volunteers must embrace evangelism and discipleship.

The pastor feels confident about coming to our teachers meetings, knowing that the teachers are all behind him. He senses that they are pulling for him, and he will pull for them. This good tension of mutual support and loyalty is a key element in our healthy atmosphere for recruitment.

A Whole Network of Spotters

+ + + + + + +

There are five of us who constitute the Christian education leadership team: the children's director, youth pastor, singles' pastor, women's ministries director, and myself. We are the main recruiters, but we involve a *whole network of lookouts for volunteers*. Even our choir members are spotters. Periodically, I ask the choir members and ushers if they have noticed people who attend regularly but are not involved. Since the choir members can scan the congregation from the choir loft, they see people who have been sitting in the same spot for weeks or months and pray for them. We have had several instances where choir members have prayed for somebody in the congregation and that person has then come off the bench and gone to work. People have come to us without knowing why and said, "I have a feeling that I need to get involved. How can I get involved?" So our choir members, ushers, and Christian education leadership team are all spotters.

Sunday school teachers are our best public relations specialists. Education workers who have had a good experience—and most of them have—are our best recruiters. They talk about ministry opportunities to other people in their classes and throughout the church family.

We receive names of prospective workers from spotters who pass the names along to us and from the *registration cards* we use each Sunday. Throughout the year, we update our congregational *computer database* where we have the names of those who have indicated their interest, experience, and desire to work. When people come two weeks in a row, they are added to our database.

Increasing Ministry Awareness

+ + + + + + +

An *annual forum* is made available to the whole church on two consecutive Sundays. (We do everything on a two-Sunday basis because we have such a high attendance turnover. Nothing is handed out for only one Sunday because it misses half the congregation.) During that forum, we provide a *booklet describing all of our regular ministry opportunities*. That booklet is also a regular part of our pastors' six-week *membership class*. I lead the session on spiritual gifts and service and use that as an opportunity to ask people to consider involvement in our Christian education program. When it is over, every new member has seen the booklet, taken a spiritual gifts inventory, and been challenged to consider possible areas of ministry.

Approaching Prospective Workers

✦ ✦ ✦ ✦ ✦ ✦ ✦

Whenever we have a hole in the youth ministry or the children's ministry, or need to replace an adult Sunday school teacher, we go to the database. We get a printout with the names of people who have indicated experience with or interest in a particular ministry. Then we talk about the need in the Christian education staff meeting and pray about it.

Let's say I am looking for an adult teacher. Now that I have a name (or names) of a prospective worker, I either go directly to that person or *make an appointment* to meet with him in a restaurant or in my office. It is an informal time when we get to know one another and share ministry philosophies and opportunities. At that time I am prepared to give him a job description and describe some of our procedures. Then I give him time to think about it— usually a week, but never longer than two weeks. I seldom use the words "pray about it," but that is what I am hoping he will do.

That brings us to a *second interview*. If he is still interested in the position we talked about a week or two earlier, I specifically discuss what is involved. I want everything said up front in this second interview so that there are no surprises. I let him know that my expectations of his involvement include more than just preparing a lesson, teaching it on Sunday, and occasionally socializing with the class members. He has to know the details of the job.

First, *we go over the job description in more detail*. Usually he will have said yes before I go into any depth on the job description. If he is hesitant but I feel that with a little more explanation he may say yes, then I continue to detail the task. If his response is a polite maybe, perhaps not wanting to disappoint me, I don't push further. Serving has to be a call of God. If I sense that his hesitation has anything to do with disappointing me, the case is closed. I don't go any farther. But if he genuinely wonders about what he is getting into, then I go on with the explanation and try to reassure him.

After detailing the job description, I spell out *the importance of participation in training opportunities*. People will not come to the teacher training sessions or special meetings if they are not told that this is part of the job. Then I present the actual teaching process.

When discussing the *time commitment*, I explain that teaching children will take maybe four or five hours a week, including teaching the class. Working with young people will take seven or eight hours a week, including calling, being out on Wednesday nights, and being with them on Sunday mornings. Teaching adults will take twelve hours a week of preparation (they prepare their own curriculum) and presentation, as well as attending class leaders' meetings.

The next step, the *observation step*, means going to classes to observe teachers in action. The prospect may be asked to help pass out papers or distribute Bibles, or he may not do anything but watch. To assist him during this step, I give him an *observation form* that guides him to look for things such as how much time the teacher talks, when she changes the tone of her voice, and how much involvement the students have. He can also watch for different teaching methodologies. If the prospect is interested in teaching children, he can observe how the teacher deals with the child who is seemingly a little out of line. He will do that observing for a couple of weeks.

During the *follow-up interview*, I ask him what he thinks. We look over the observation form, answer any of his questions, and make sure he understands his responsibilities. We talk over any questions or fears he may have. Based on his concerns, I frequently provide a *resource*, such as a video, to help allay those concerns. I go over how to use the curriculum, both its preparation and presentation, especially with those who will work with children. When the prospective worker voices a willingness to assume a teaching role, I ask him to complete a volunteer application.

None of these meetings lasts over an hour. If the prospective worker has come this far, he has filled out the application, completed the observation step, and had his questions answered. If his answer is still yes, then I have an assignment for him.

Protecting Our Children

＋ ＋ ＋ ＋ ＋ ＋ ＋

There is another point that is critical to the recruitment of volunteers. Our culture and society require that we deal with the issue of child abuse. So far we have not had a problem with this in our church, but I always introduce it during the first meeting that I have with prospective volunteers and go into it in more detail in the second interview.

There are *three key questions* we ask prospective volunteers on the application. The first question inquires whether they have any handicaps. Largely that is for involvement with children, especially areas where they may have to lift children. The next question asks if they have ever been convicted or accused of any domestic violence, abuse, or crime related to children. If they answer "yes," they have to cite what their involvement was. It is something that our lawyers have told us is helpful and not discriminatory. Our third question has to do with whether they have a criminal record. We require everyone who works with minors, children, and youth to complete this question.

We follow through with a *criminal record check*. We also check their *references*. In the event that we were to have any problems with a volunteer, we could show that we were not negligent and the volunteer had been thoroughly checked out. If there was any false information, it was on the volunteer's end and not the church's.

The prospective workers bring back the form to the second interview. We have had a few people who have questioned, "Do I have to fill this out?" It is troublesome to them. But when we give them examples of situations in other southern California churches, no one has refused to do it. Once they understand the rationale for it, that it is for the protection of our children and the church, they gladly answer the questions.

Since we have performed criminal record and reference checks on the lead teachers, we do not require the same background checks for those who serve on a rotation basis, such as parents in the nursery. However, we do ask them to fill out the application form because we want the rotation parents who are working in the nursery, toddlers, and creepers rooms to be aware that we are watching and there are guidelines. This has been well-received by parents because it gives them a sense of security, so we have not had any resistance to signing the form. This is something new for us. Our whole staff has signed on; now it's a process of having new people do the same.

A One-Year Commitment

+ + + + + + +

When recruiting teachers, we don't talk of commitments longer than one year, but silently we are praying that they will be with us for a long time. Normally we don't take anybody on for less than three months, unless of course, they are doing a short-term assignment. Adult Sunday school teachers are encouraged to teach at least forty-two Sundays a year. During the summer, we continue to have classes except the sixth grade, which joins the junior high class for the summer. So anybody who is a sixth-grade teacher only serves nine months out of the year; otherwise, teaching is a twelve-month commitment.

We make note of when a teacher comes on, which is not always in September. When it comes close to the anniversary date, we arrange to have an interview with her. If she is doing well, we celebrate and ask how she feels about this opportunity. If we are happy with her and she stays on, then we have a teacher for another year. But if she says, "I have done my year. I feel good about it, but I think that I need to be with my husband in adult Sunday school," that's fine. We praise the Lord with her, pray with her, and say thank you. *We give her the option to return when she is ready*. Maybe she can come and help for a week, or can help in another short-term opportunity such as Vacation Bible School, camp counseling, or substitute teaching. On the other hand, if we have had good communication and sense that this ministry "fit" just isn't right, we will both know it and we can have an amicable separation or reassignment to another area. If we need to find a replacement, we try to have a lead time of two months before the end of her tenure.

Staying in Touch With Their Peers

+ + + + + + +

At Sierra Madre, we are concerned that teachers maintain contact with their own adult peers. We do several things to *encourage identity with their life-stage groups*. First, we alert their adult Sunday school classes that they are teaching, making sure their names remain on class rosters. We urge their Sunday school classes to invite them to any extra activities or social events and to maintain a shepherding relationship with the teacher, which is a very satisfying thing for the volunteer. It keeps the teachers' identity and relationships with their adult classes alive.

We also challenge the class to adopt the children or youth that their class member is teaching as a missions/prayer project. As a result, virtually every class has an *adult class that is praying for the teachers and students*. It provides relational ties to the church at large. Occasionally, teachers may even bring their class to their adult class to sing a song or quote a verse. Of course, that is always a big event. With our multiple services, that doesn't always work out, but when it does, there is a positive response.

Supporting Our Volunteers

+ + + + + + +

There is one other important thing that I share with prospective teachers. I have three things that I feel are important to my job when it comes to these volunteers. I call them my three "S's."

The first "s" is *support*. I am here to support them. Whether it is children's workers or youth workers, they are going to get the benefit of the doubt in any kind of sticky situation. If it comes out that they were wrong, we will deal with it. But I am here to support them.

The second "s" is *supply*. Their service shouldn't cost them their own money. It might cost them time. It might cost them some stress. It might cost them some sleep. But it should not cost them any money. We try to provide whatever they need including curriculum, resources, and training. A good example of support and training we provide are our SALT meetings—Sunday school, Adult, Leaders, and Teachers meetings—which we have four times a year. Our logo is a salt shaker. At these meetings, we have a time of vision casting. We talk about our goals and the church. We talk about something that should stretch us. We provide skills training using videos, demonstrations, or any number of things. And sometimes we just have the teachers talk about the things they are doing to encourage one another.

Third, and here we stretch the alliteration, is *"selebration."* This has two dimensions: evaluation and appreciation. Each evaluation is a kind of celebration of the good things that God has done in and through their ministry. For me, it's a celebration even when we talk about areas where they are lacking and I can help with those growth areas.

We even view the close of a service assignment as a celebration. If this teacher is not the right person for the job, we will have had enough contact that she knows where we are coming from. It is a mutual decision to end that teaching or volunteer situation. Maybe it is just that someone is not a third-grade teacher and ought to be working in another area of ministry. Because of our efforts to clearly communicate with volunteers from the beginning, I have had few problems releasing people from a specific task or reassigning them. I have only had problems when the explanations and expectations were poorly communicated and it was a surprise to the teacher.

"Selebration" is also appreciation. We try to express appreciation to our people both individually and corporately. We try to remember them with thank-you notes, or words of appreciation and pictures in our biweekly communications piece. We list teachers' names in the bulletin and remember their birthdays. On the second Sunday in September, we celebrate our public, private, and Sunday school teachers by including all of them in the same prayer. We have never had anyone upset to be included in prayer with our volunteer Sunday school teachers. They have something in common as Christian educators, and the recognition is appreciated by all. So at least two or three times a year, all of our teachers will get some recognition. I don't think you could find a happier bunch of teachers.

Christian teaching is an educational endeavor that has no graduation point. It has a coronation; we die and go to Heaven. But we do not have a graduation the way we do at the end of twelve years of school or four years of college. The best type of graduation for any student is to move from just learning about God to serving God when the Spirit nudges and says, "It's time." It's great to be nearby as a Christian education director to help that student "graduate."

If there's a key word to describe the philosophy of volunteerism at Sierra Madre Congregational Church, it is atmosphere. The atmosphere that permeates this church is that "every member is a minister." Anyone who attends SMCC for even a modest amount of time is impressed with the concept that the average Christian serves. In this type of environment, people are not surprised to be asked to consider a specific ministry in the church. In fact, if no one offered you an opportunity to serve, you might wonder if something was wrong with you. Any congregation that can develop this type of healthy atmosphere for volunteerism will find more people responding affirmatively to invitations to minister.

Ministry Resources

The following materials are used at Sierra Madre Congregational Church in their Christian education ministries. Permission to use and adapt these resources in your congregation is granted. Duplication or distribution of these copyrighted materials for resale is prohibited.

APPLICATION FOR CHILDREN'S/YOUTH MINISTRY (CONFIDENTIAL)

This is part of the application process to be completed by all applicants for any position (volunteer or compensated) involving the supervision or custody of minors. The purpose of this part of the process is to further ensure a safe and secure environment for those children and youth entrusted by God to the ministries of SMCC and who use our facilities. We must ask you some personal questions, which are unfortunately essential in today's world. Your responses will be kept confidential within the pastoral staff and commission related to the recruiting process. (If your responses exceed the space provided, please use the back side of each sheet.)

Today's Date: _____ Home Phone: _____

Work Phone: _____

Name _____

Present Address _____

Marital Status _____ Social Security # _____

Member of SMCC? Yes _____ No _____ If no, where? _____

What type of children's/youth ministry do you prefer? _____

_____

What do you bring to the children's/youth ministry with which you wish to work? (spiritual, skills, experience, training, etc.) _____

_____

_____

On what date are you available? _____

Maximum length of your commitment _____

> *Your honest responses to the following questions will help assure our church family, parents, and children of the finest staff and care we can provide. Your affirmative response, if necessary, does not automatically disqualify you from the joy of service, but will help us better know how to work with you and support you in service should you be placed.*

1. Have you any physical handicaps or conditions preventing you from performing the activities related to children's/youth work? Yes _____ No _____ If yes, please explain:

   _____

   _____

2. Have you ever been convicted or accused of any domestic violence, child abuse, child molestation, or any other crime related to children or youth? Yes _____ No _____ If yes, please explain:

   _____

   _____

3. I authorize the church to obtain a state-provided criminal records check if it is thought to be important, so long as the results are kept confidential. Yes _____ No _____

(continued)

I have read the attached procedures for working with minors at SMCC and pledge to support them as I minister. Yes _____ No _____

List other churches you have attended regularly during the past seven years. (If no churches, please list any schools and organizations where you have worked with children or youth.)

Church Name   1. _____   2. _____
Street Address   _____   _____
City/State/Zip   _____   _____
Years Attended   _____   _____

Type of children's or youth ministry you did:

   _____   _____
   _____   _____
   _____   _____
   _____   _____

List at least two personal references who are not former co-workers or relatives.
Name   1. _____   2. _____
Street Address   _____   _____
City/State/Zip   _____   _____
Telephone   _____   _____

Personal Commitment

The information contained in this personal reference form is correct to the best of my knowledge. *I authorize any references or churches listed in this application to give you any information (including opinions) that they may have regarding my character and fitness for children's/youth work.* I release all such references from any liability for furnishing such evaluations to you, provided they do so in good faith and without malice. I waive any right that I may have to inspect references provided on my behalf.

Should my application be accepted, I agree to be bound by the bylaws and policies of Sierra Madre Congregational Church, and to refrain from unscriptural conduct in the performance of my services on behalf of the church. Sierra Madre Congregational Church commits to supporting you in your appointment with affirming supervision and ongoing training, as together we serve Jesus Christ and share in His love with our children and youth.

Applicant's Signature _____ Date _____

Witness _____ Date _____
           (Departmental minister)

(Bylaws and policies of Sierra Madre Congregational Church are available in the business office.)

PROCEDURES FOR VOLUNTEERS WORKING WITH MINORS

All volunteers in children's or youth ministry are subject to the supervision and evaluation of the child-care coordinator, children's minister, youth minister, and Christian education commission. SMCC reserves the right to dismiss volunteers who are unscriptural in conduct or fail to follow the policies for volunteers working with minors.

All volunteers in children's or youth ministries must be personally interviewed by the respective minister in their area of desired service. The interview process includes completing an application that deals with some of the critical social issues of our world. The application is confidential and is used to help our church provide a safe and secure environment for the children and youth who participate in our programs and use our facilities.

Below are procedures volunteers are asked to comply with to prevent allegations of **child abuse** or to prevent the actual occurrence of child abuse.

1. It is recommended that every group of children or youth have at least two workers present at all times. (At times, this is difficult, but having another adult present is your best protection against false allegations.) It is a good rule to never be alone with a young person. (SMCC adheres to minimum leader-child/youth ratios.)

2. It is also recommended that window blinds and doors be kept open in classrooms where children's activities are occurring. Try not to be put in what could be termed a compromising position.

3. Physical contact with children should be minimal. In kindergarten and below, some appropriate touching and hugging is permissible. However, this should only be done in the presence of other adults in an open classroom. In grades 1–12, physical contact should be given with extreme care. It is recommended that a volunteer should not display physical affection to a young person of the opposite gender.

4. When taking children to the rest room, volunteers should only supervise children of the same gender. It is recommended that, if possible, two adults remain in the rest room with the children. Children should have as much privacy as possible when using the rest room. Workers should enter a rest room stall only when absolutely necessary to assist a child.

5. All activities or outings outside the normal planned children's or youth ministry calendar must be approved by the appropriate minister to ensure proper supervision, e.g., Sunday school teachers or group leaders initiating a special activity for their group.

(continued)

6. Visitors or "new volunteers" are not permitted to help in children's ministry unless approved by the children's minister or child-care coordinator.

7. Parents are permitted to observe their child in his or her class. However, parents must notify the department leader or program director of their presence. At no time are parents allowed to be alone with any child except their own. They are only to observe the class or activity they desire.

8. Volunteers should never drive a child home alone without another adult in the car. In the event it is necessary, the child(ren's) parent(s) should be notified beforehand and permission granted.

As volunteers, there are two other important areas of which you want to be informed. **Health expectations and emergency procedures** in the event of fire or earthquake are considerations that every volunteer worker should know.

1. In the children's ministry, the health guidelines are in the handbook as well as posted in every preschool room. Know the expectations. Help prevent the unnecessary spread of disease.

2. Every room on the SMCC campus has an emergency exit sign. Procedure flyers are also available. Know what you should do in the room you are working in the event of a fire or earthquake.

3. First aid kits are placed in each major children's/youth center and their locations are clearly noted. Become familiar with their locations and contents.

The staff and leadership of Sierra Madre Congregational Church are grateful to God for the faithful service of the marvelous volunteers He has given us to minister to the babies, toddlers, children, and youth that are a vital part of this fellowship. *We as leaders covenant to support our volunteers in prayer and through training in identifying abuse and how our volunteers can protect themselves from accusations of abuse, as well as how to deal with disease and emergencies. These procedures are part of that process.*

Chapter Two

Getting to Know You: A Relational Approach

First Assembly of God
San Diego, California

Imagine yourself sitting in a worship service hearing your pastor talk about the importance of ministry to children. In fact, he frequently mentions that the church needs its very best people working with its next generation. The pastor asks the best theologians to serve in the children's program. And to prove that the church places its highest value on its children, once a year a special announcement and commitment card are placed in the pew soliciting volunteers for the children's ministry only. Well, welcome to First Assembly of God in San Diego, California. Children's pastor, Jay Hostetler, tells us about this remarkable ministry.

Relational Ministry

✝ ✝ ✝ ✝ ✝ ✝ ✝

There are two things that I think are really important for recruiting volunteers. The first is that I model *personal involvement in teaching*. In the past, the church has had some administrative type of recruiters who just filled in the slots. They lacked a hands-on approach to ministry. So when I came here thirteen years ago as minister to children, the first thing I did was to take an active role in leadership. At that time I directed the children's church program. I wanted people to see that I was interested and involved in doing ministry myself. People learn by example, so as they saw me getting involved, it became easier to recruit people to join in.

The second thing that is really important to me, and I think it is one of my strengths, is the *relational base of ministry*. I spend a lot of time with people in restaurants, on golf courses, sharing my vision and articulating ministry goals. I'm always building relationships. Why? Because even though we do the same things other churches do, such as membership surveys, pulpit announcements and focused presentations, our recruitment effectiveness seems to come down to having relationships with people. Because of these relationships, I am able to say to a person, "Come alongside and help us."

I need to *model relationship building* with my people if I want them to build relationships with children. Our whole philosophy of recruiting is based on the philosophy of relationships. Procedurally, that's important for me. To me, the relational side of recruiting in churches has often been overlooked. Some church leaders tend to be more task-oriented, more ministry description-oriented. I do those things, too, but if my focus is only on the task and not on the person, then I will always end up with a system that is just nuts and bolts. It's not going to be focused on ministry to the kids.

Personal invitations are critical to the growth of our volunteer staff. I don't want people to serve the children just because they have a relationship with me, but at the same time, it seems to work when we're friends and I know them well enough that I can anticipate some of their needs.

Longevity in ministry is also a real advantage in the recruitment of volunteers. With longevity we build credibility and enlarge our relational nets, which has been a real plus for us. I have been at First Assembly for thirteen years; our senior minister has served for twenty-eight years; many of our key leaders have served for multiple years.

The longer we are in a particular church, the easier it is to *identify various recruiting pools*.

Right now we're experiencing a growing recruiting pool among senior adults. Many seniors have both time and financial reserves, and are investing themselves in ministry. Young couples who are considering having children are another great recruiting pool. Young parents are a mixed bag: some are too busy to help, others want a change of pace when they come to church, while still others make some of our best workers.

The whole relational side of recruiting volunteers has not been emphasized enough. Yet this is how we can draw the most people who will serve for the right reasons. We can do large campaigns and get people to serve out of guilt, but those people usually end up serving for only a few months. Then they decide it just isn't what they want to do. But when we are getting to know people on a relational basis, we have a better chance of *matching their skill level to a ministry need*. Then we will have them for the long term. I have some people who have served with me every year for the entire thirteen years that I have been here.

Retention Is the Key

+ + + + + + +

I don't want to be seen as some kind of professional headhunter, but as a person who moves among the flock and cares for them. I've always tried to get involved in what my volunteers are doing to the extent that if I'm not teaching a class, I'll walk around and *make sure that teacher needs are met* and they're happy with what they are doing. It amazes me that some pastors don't realize that it is the *retention* of volunteers that is the key to staffing.

At First Assembly, we minister to about five hundred children on Sunday mornings. Fortunately, we maintain an 80 to 85 percent retention rate with our staff from year to year. Obviously that makes my job of recruiting a lot easier than a pastor with 30 to 50 percent turnover each year. When I have to recruit only 15 percent new staff, our whole ministry runs more smoothly.

It is also interesting to note that with my long tenure at First Assembly, I have run through an entire cycle of parents: Parents of now high school- and college-aged kids are still teaching and I once recruited them to work in the nursery. I have the benefit of some mature people who still work in the system but who have moved on to assist with their teenagers and college-aged kids in specific ministries. The longevity side of retention has tremendous benefits.

As the primary person responsible for recruitment, it's beneficial to *meet as many people as possible*. For example, it's important for me to know the parents of younger children, so I teach a young couple's class even though as the children's pastor, I have full responsibility on Sundays for the children's program. *Teaching a class affords new relationships* with younger adults, and I am getting to know their children. This is also a tremendous recruiting pool. Without even asking, these people have come and asked, "Do you need help?"

We do not limit our recruitment to members only. We have people serving in ministry leadership who are not yet members. We encourage people to pursue membership, but we have never felt it was essential to serving. Some churches have particular requirements regarding membership, but we have a rather open policy. We encourage attendees to become members, but it is not mandatory in order for them to serve in the children's ministry program. If they have been around a while, we have records of their involvement level.

We note when people first become active at First Assembly through our *computer records*. We become better acquainted with many of them as they get more involved in our programs. If there is somebody that I don't know or haven't seen around, I rely on our leadership for a reference. Frequently another leader knows the person from a study group, a counseling situation, or another service area. I'll ask his opinion of that person—what has he observed? We have a pretty good pastoral and leadership network that helps us with backgrounds.

Discovering People's Ministry Interests

+ + + + + + +

The first part of every year, we take a *ministry census* throughout the church. A ministry form is distributed during both of our Sunday morning services, and we actually take the time during the service to fill this out. The form covers ministries and areas where they feel gifted, including ministries with children, youth, adults, and so on. I have had as many as eighty and as few as thirty people indicate interest in working in children's ministries.

Once a quarter we have a *membership seminar*. The various ministries of the church are introduced in the sessions, and we get prospects from that recruitment pool as well.

Hospitality/informational calls are a third way we learn about the interests of potential volunteers. Every person who visits our church is sent a follow-up letter. An enclosed form asks questions such as, "Do you have interest in the children's ministry program?" These new or recent attenders are encouraged to return the survey via the self-addressed stamped envelope. These forms are entirely for informational purposes and we don't violate that by using it as a recruiting tool. However, say, for example, that I'm talking to a person on the phone and tell them, "Here is the information on our children's choir." If they respond with, "You know, at my other church I was involved with the children's choir and wondered if it was possible to get involved here," well, of course I'm more than eager to help them! Hospitality calls are not primarily recruiting calls; they are informational calls. But they often lead to questions about involvement, which gives us another opportunity to recruit.

A fourth stream in our recruiting process is the utilization of *a children's ministry announcement*. Each year in May we invite people to consider working with our children. This invitation is for children's workers only, not volunteers in general. The three-week campaign has only one pulpit announcement, and then we leave response cards in the pew racks for three Sundays. The completed cards can be placed in an offering plate. This public announcement has been very successful for us, and every year has led to a number of new contacts. We've written blurbs in the general church newsletter, but we don't get much response from that.

We can do that focused announcement on Sunday morning because our senior pastor visibly supports our children's ministry. That is probably what drew me to him thirteen years ago. He stands behind me and has always said that recruiting is *our* responsibility—it's not just my responsibility. He has been very involved with recruiting and will often make the initial announcement that sets off this three-week campaign. When he personally makes that announcement, it carries an enormous amount of clout with the church fellowship.

This endorsement for children's ministries is permitted because no other ministry in the church is responsible for the number of volunteers that we need, though a close second may be the music ministry because of the need for orchestra and choir people. Because children's ministry utilizes a full staff for both Sunday morning services and the Wednesday night programs, we're looking at numbers that are larger than what anybody else on staff is managing.

The Benefit of Team Teaching

+ + + + + + +

For both healthy teacher-student relationships and good classroom management, we work toward having *low teacher-student ratios*. We aim for ratios in early childhood of about 1 to 4, and a ratio of 1 to 6 in elementary. We have come pretty close to those ratios, but we have more difficulty finding volunteers to work in early childhood than with older children. Perhaps some mistakenly view this work as child care rather than ministry. Still, we try to stay as close to the ratios as we can.

Team teaching gives us a bit more flexibility. We can lower our ratios by having, for lack of a better term, nonskilled children's ministry personnel assisting. Sometimes these are people who are just investigating the possibility of working in a particular program. We place them in a classroom for two or three weeks with the regular teachers. This yields a better teacher-student ratio and helps people come into the system. Team teaching also allows us to utilize teenagers with our experienced workers. This has proven to be a great way to turn some of those kids on to ministry. Over time, many have become lead teachers themselves.

Personal Interviews

+ + + + + + +

Every time I interview volunteers, I come out of those interviews with a ministry profile. This is not entered into the computer at this point. It is a paper copy consisting of their ministry survey and my notes. We ask prospective workers to complete the survey and bring it to the interview we have together. Sometimes they have questions or uncompleted areas. We simply finish those in my office.

To ensure that we have a good mixture of people, I'm constantly looking at those files and asking, "How does this person match up with that person? Would this be a team that would work well together?" As the process continues, I probably go through every single profile twice a week.

By the time I'm done with that process, I have over two hundred profiles in my file, and a pretty good feeling about who's going to serve where. That information is gleaned out of the personal interviews I conduct each year with every prospective worker and returning volunteer. I go over that information repeatedly, making sure that we put people in the right places. The actual placement of people doesn't occur until I have talked to everybody. Then a final decision is made about ministry assignments.

A Heart for Kids

+ + + + + +

I really want to find people who have a heart for children. We can train people to work with children, but we cannot train them to have a heart for kids. I try to communicate to the volunteers how we can make an impact on the next generation.

When I first came to First Assembly, I told people that within a short time, prospective volunteers would have to be placed on a waiting list. We haven't reached that point yet, though we have come close on a couple of occasions. Obviously, we would never have anybody wait; we would find a place for them to serve. But I believe that when we invite people to work in the church, we often go about it all wrong. Unfortunately, the emphasis is, "I hope you will do this because we really can't find anybody else who will."

By contrast, when we *raise the expectations* and tell people it is a privilege to work with kids, they value service. At First Assembly, we have worked hard to raise the standard and let people know that working with kids is a privilege. We don't take just anybody. We only take people who are willing to make a difference in the lives of children. This attitude communicates a whole different philosophy to people.

Our senior pastor is constantly encouraging me and saying that the best theologians in the church need to be working in the children's program. When he says that publicly, it means a lot and tells people that *we want our very best people working with kids*. We want disciplined, spiritual people who are interested in making a difference in the lives of kids.

Through all of the networking we do and the relationships we develop, we try to establish the value that if you are a part of our children's ministry, you are participating in a high calling. You have been screened, you've been talked to specifically about your role, and you are a special person because you are sharing your life with God's children.

+ + + + + + +

During President Clinton's first presidential campaign, he had one slogan plastered all over his offices: "It's the economy, Stupid." He wanted to make sure he remembered the main thing that was of concern to the American people. In a similar way, those of us who are involved in Christian ministry would benefit by remembering: "It's relationships, Stupid." Okay, perhaps we shouldn't call ourselves stupid, but frequently we act as if the main thing is the programming.

The effective volunteer ministry at First Assembly of God in San Diego is attributed primarily to the networking of relationships built by their executive leadership. People are leery of a professional headhunter who is trying to fill a slot with their body. But they trust a friend whose heart they know, who offers an invitation to invest their lives in meaningful ministry.

The old Fram Filter commercial used to say: "You can pay me now or you can pay me later." Jay Hostetler and the team at First Assembly of God prefer to spend their time up front making sure they place the right people in the right ministry job. Yet their investment on the front end—relationship building and interviewing—pays off with an astounding 85 percent retention rate of their teachers. Churches that do this initial type of relationship building, as well as caring for their volunteers throughout their tenure, will build an effective team of volunteer leaders.

Ministry Resources

The following materials are used at First Assembly of God in San Diego in their Christian education ministries. Permission to use and adapt these resources in your congregation is granted. Duplication or distribution of these copyrighted materials for resale is prohibited.

CHILDREN'S MINISTRY PROFILE

Appointment: _____
                        Date   Time

Date: _____

Name: _____ Address: _____

City/State: _____ Zip: _____ Day Phone: _____

Areas Checked: _____

Target Area: _____

Brief Personal History: _____

_____

_____

Church History: _____

_____

_____

Why involvement with children? _____

_____

_____

Share your gifts that might be helpful in children's ministry: _____

_____

_____

Explain: Length of commitment _____

             Planning responsibilities _____

             Team Life responsibilities _____

                 Ministry _____

                 Social _____

             Preservice mechanism _____

MINISTRY SURVEY FOR CHILDREN'S/YOUTH DEPARTMENT

This survey is to be completed by all those desiring any ministry position (volunteer or compensated) involving the supervision or custody of minors. It is being used to help the church provide a safe and secure environment for those children and youth who participate in our programs and use our facilities.

GENERAL

Name _____ Date _____
        Last   *First*   *Middle Initial*

Address _____
        Number   *Street*   *City*   *Zip*

Number of years at this address _____ If less than five, give previous address and number of

years at that address: Years _____ Address _____

Occupation _____

Social Security No. _____ Driver's License No. _____ ❑ Verified

Marital status: ❑ Married   ❑ Single   ❑ Separated   ❑ Divorced   ❑ Widowed

Home phone _____ Phone during day _____

Are you a Christian? _____

How long have you had a personal relationship with Jesus Christ? _____

Have you been baptized in the Holy Spirit? _____

Have you been baptized by water immersion? _____ If so, where? _____

How long have you attended First Assembly? _____

Are you a member? _____ If so, how long? _____

Please check those services that you regularly attend at First Assembly:
     Sunday   ❑ 9:00 A.M.   Wednesday   ❑ 7:00 P.M
               ❑ 10:45 A.M.
               ❑ 6:00 P.M.

What area of Christian service do you desire to be involved in? _____

Please explain why you feel God's call on your life for this area of service.

(continued)

CHURCH ACTIVITY

What leadership experience have you had?

List all previous church work or other work involving children and youth (identify place and type of work). List supervisors.

What other churches have you attended regularly during the past five years?

List any gifts, training, education, or other factors that have prepared you for children's/youth work.

PERSONAL REFERENCES

Name _____   Name _____

Address _____   Address _____

_____   _____

Phone _____   Phone _____

PERSONAL HISTORY

Have you ever been convicted for the use or sale of drugs? _____
If yes, please explain:

Have you ever been hospitalized or treated for alcohol or substance abuse? _____
If yes, please explain:

(continued)

Have you ever been arrested for a criminal offense excluding minor traffic violations? _____
If yes, please explain:

Have you ever been accused, arrested, or convicted of any sexually related crimes? _____
If yes, please explain:

Have you ever been accused, arrested, or convicted of any abuse-related actions? _____
If yes, please explain:

Are there any circumstances involving your lifestyle or your background that would call into question your being entrusted with the care of young people?

APPLICANT'S STATEMENT

The information contained in this application is correct to the best of my knowledge. I authorize any references, churches, or other organizations listed in this application to give you any information they may have regarding my character and fitness for children's/youth work, and I release all such references from liability for any damage that may result from furnishing such evaluations to you.

Should my application be accepted, I agree to be bound by the Articles and Bylaws and Policies of First Assembly of God, San Diego, California, and to refrain from unscriptural conduct in the performance of my services on behalf of the church.

I understand that the personal information will be held confidential by the professional church staff.

Applicant's signature _____ Date _____

Received by department head _____ Date _____

Applicant interviewed by _____ Date _____

MINISTRY INVOLVEMENT UPDATE

Serving Together at San Diego First Assembly

From him the whole body, joined and held together by every supporting ligament, grows and builds itself up in love, as each part does its work. (Ephesians 4:16)

Name _____

Street/City/Zip _____

Phone—home _____ Phone—work/other _____

Birthdate (mo/day/yr) _____ Today's date _____

PLEASE CHECK AS MANY IN EACH COLUMN AS APPLY.

Spiritual Gifts

❑ Serving
❑ Teaching
❑ Leadership
❑ Giving
❑ Mercy & Caring
❑ Evangelism
❑ Encouraging
❑ Other _____

Fan into flame the gift of God, which is in you. (2 Timothy 1:6)

Areas of Interest

AGE LEVEL
❑ Preschool/Nursery
❑ Grade School
❑ Junior High
❑ High School
❑ College
❑ Adults 20s–30s
❑ Adults 40s–50s
❑ Senior Adults (Adults 55+)
❑ Any/All Adult Ages

MINISTRY AREA
❑ Ushering & Greeting
❑ Information Center
❑ Choir, Orchestra & Productions
❑ Sound & Lights
❑ Singles
❑ Couples
❑ Home Fellowships
❑ Support & Recovery Groups
❑ Other _____

Carry each other's burdens, and in this way you will fulfill the law of Christ. (Galatians 6:2)

Talents & Availability

❑ Musical Instrument
❑ Singing
❑ Writing
❑ Decorating
❑ Sound or Lights Technician
❑ Small Group Facilitator
❑ General Facility Maintenance
❑ Tape Duplication
❑ Hospitality
❑ Traffic Direction
❑ Clerical or Data Entry
❑ General Serving
❑ Drawing/Painting
❑ Visiting
❑ Prayer
❑ Teacher's Assistant
❑ Mentoring
❑ Photography
❑ Van/Bus Driver
❑ Graphic Arts
❑ Desktop Publishing
❑ Other _____

Whatever you do, do it all for the glory of God. (1 Corinthians 10:31)

How This Survey Is Used

The information is entered into the church's records and is made available only to pastors and ministry leaders of First Assembly.

This data is used only on an "as needed" basis. If you desire immediate involvement in a ministry area, please contact the ministry's leaders.

Your response indicates your willingness to be contacted in regard to a ministry need. It does not obligate you to service.

Thank you!

I'll Say Yes

I would like to talk to pastor Jay about involvement in the children's program.

Name: _____

Phone: Day _____

Evening _____

❏ Kids Camp Prayer Partners
❏ Serve on Wednesday
❏ Serve on Sunday
❏ Serve in Child Care Center
(once every six weeks)

I'll Say Yes

I would like to talk to pastor Jay about involvement in the children's program.

Name: _____

Phone: Day _____

Evening _____

❏ Kids Camp Prayer Partners
❏ Serve on Wednesday
❏ Serve on Sunday
❏ Serve in Child Care Center
(once every six weeks)

I'll Say Yes

I would like to talk to pastor Jay about involvement in the children's program.

Name: _____

Phone: Day _____

Evening _____

❏ Kids Camp Prayer Partners
❏ Serve on Wednesday
❏ Serve on Sunday
❏ Serve in Child Care Center
(once every six weeks)

I'll Say Yes

I would like to talk to pastor Jay about involvement in the children's program.

Name: _____

Phone: Day _____

Evening _____

❏ Kids Camp Prayer Partners
❏ Serve on Wednesday
❏ Serve on Sunday
❏ Serve in Child Care Center
(once every six weeks)

Chapter Three

There's a Place for You: A Systemic Approach

Bay Leaf Baptist Church
Raleigh, North Carolina

It's hard to be a spectator at Bay Leaf Baptist Church in Raleigh, North Carolina. Even if you've been at the church for only a few weeks, someone is likely to approach you to see if you'd assist with a ministry assignment. Oh, you wouldn't immediately be thrust into a major activity, such as teaching your own Sunday school class, but you would be invited to be part of a ministry team to serve within their fellowship.

Bay Leaf's congregation-wide, decentralized approach to inviting volunteers to minister is a significant factor in the high energy level of this growing congregation. Pastor Will Gatling, minister of education, tells us more about the Bay Leaf story.

Everybody's Doing Something

+ + + + + + +

Not everybody can teach, but everybody can serve in some capacity. When I meet a person who suggests that they can't do a particular thing in the church, I view it as my responsibility to help them see other possibilities. If they say "I can't do this" or "I'm not willing to do that," I keep offering options. I ask, "What about this?" or "What about that?"

Our church divides work among many committees. Sometimes a committee gets so large that it becomes unmanageable. When that happens, we have people who are just wasting their time. Part of my responsibility is to subdivide work, which means I actually develop more volunteer positions in order to provide meaningful service opportunities so that everyone can serve somewhere. All Christians need to serve in some ministry. Their ministry has to be something that they can feel good about and be successful at doing.

We have a *system for inviting people to volunteer*. It's not put down on paper per se, but we have a general attitude. Throughout the year, but specifically in the springtime, our pastor preaches about our conviction that everyone should serve in some volunteer capacity. That may be as simple as serving on a committee or taking the offering. It may be teaching a Bible study class or serving as a deacon. But we emphasize that having everyone involved somewhere is important to us.

That same philosophy is woven through the teaching that takes place in our *new member class*. This is a four-week class conducted every three months for anyone who comes into our congregation seeking membership. It is held during the Sunday school hour, which is a convenient time for people to attend. It gives prospective members a chance to become acquainted with us as a church and as Southern Baptists, and also offers them opportunities for service. They are exposed to the many ways in which they can become involved. They also learn that all members are expected to actively serve.

A general rule in Southern Baptist life is that you have to be a church member for about a year before you can have a ministry responsibility. At Bay Leaf, we don't subscribe to that. Basically, if people have been in the church for three or four months, we can put them to work. They must go through an interview with me first to provide a little bit of background about themselves. Nonmembers are also allowed to sing in choir and serve on some committees; for example, they can serve on our Fall Festival committee, which is our alternative to Halloween, or work in a nonteaching position in Vacation Bible School.

We are careful, however, not to place newcomers into solo teaching situations. All of our children's classes—preschool, children, and youth—utilize team teaching. Adult classes are led by couples. While I don't give new members who've been here only thirty days their own Sunday school class, I allow those who want to serve to assist in an area where there is a team already in place. I don't give people a full-time teaching position immediately because they need time to become acclimated to our congregation. However, if they volunteer, we allow them to come into our church and begin serving almost immediately. We have found that an open door to service is the best way to involve the whole church in ministry.

Filling Our Volunteer Positions

+ + + + + + +

We enlist people in a couple of different ways. One way is through our *nominating committee*, which is made up of lay people who have the responsibility of filling the volunteer positions in our church. It's ultimately their responsibility, but I serve as the staff liaison with them.

The nominating committee has an intense period of work from March through July with the purpose of enlisting people for the fall. The rest of the year, they are "on call" with me because we start new Sunday school classes all year long and have volunteer positions to fill. When we have new people who want to work in a particular area, I go back to that committee for their approval.

We begin finding people through an *annual survey* of our congregation. We distribute a ministries survey for several weeks in our Sunday school classes and during the worship services. We prefer to print the information rather than merely announcing it from the pulpit because the survey gives people a chance to see the variety of ministry opportunities available in our church.

The nominating committee collects the completed surveys. They begin the recruiting process by listing all of our program leaders, such as the women's missionary director, men's ministry director, Sunday school director, and so on. Next, they chip away at the ministry openings within those programs. Week by week, as we try to fill those needs, we go back to the nominating committee for coordination purposes. This enables us to manage our recruitment efforts not only within my areas, but in the youth ministry, music ministry, and other programs.

We have found that people enjoy *teaming for ministry*. At Bay Leaf, we have about thirty-six committees, and I work with a large number of those committees. We have committees that work on projects that happen only once a year, such as the homecoming committee and Fall Festival committee. The Vacation Bible School committee works diligently for five months. After Vacation Bible School, they disband for the next seven months. We also have ongoing committees like the people who put flowers in our sanctuary, the personnel committee, and the stewardship committee.

Our leaders are allowed to enlist their own workers. Say Mrs. Brown is working with the Fall Festival. She is a good friend of Mrs. Smith and would like to work with her, so I allow her to ask Mrs. Smith to serve on that committee. The drawback to this is that less active members can be overlooked. The nominating committee, which serves as our clearinghouse, helps us with balance. The committee's responsibility is to keep focusing on those surveys so they spread the responsibilities over the entire congregation. This way Mrs. Smith won't be nominated to twenty-five tasks, while someone else is overlooked.

As in many Southern Baptist churches, we need the *support of the pastor* for something to be successful. If we want any program to be staffed, we need the pastor's support. Even though we usually don't want to take time on Sunday mornings to talk about those ministries, sometimes a word during his sermon about the ministry is helpful. Or sometimes it involves a short note from the pastor in the newsletter. People want to hear that the senior pastor is for this. They don't want to buy into it if he doesn't.

Working With a Point System

✝ ✝ ✝ ✝ ✝ ✝ ✝

Our church utilizes a *point system* as the framework for managing our volunteers. Every ministry position in the church is rated by points. *Three-point positions* meet every week and require the most amount of time, for instance, serving as a deacon, Sunday school teacher, or missions teacher. *Two-point positions* meet monthly or seasonally, like VBS, and will have an intense work period for four or five months. A team of fifteen men and women leads our Vacation Bible School. It's a big program in our church, and each summer we impact about five hundred children through this ministry. The people who lead VBS are in the two-point category because they work intensely in the springtime with training sessions and preparations. Activities that meet occasionally but require very little preparation are *one-point positions*. Serving on the flower committee or ushering team falls within this category.

Our goal is that no volunteer have more than seven points. Our purpose is twofold: first, we want to get more people serving and fewer people doing too many things; but more importantly, we prefer that people have only one teaching assignment. If someone teaches Sunday school, we don't want them teaching Wednesday night missions too. There are some exceptions to this rule because we have Sunday school teachers who will teach a short-term discipleship training class on Sunday night for four or six weeks. On occasion, a person may teach twice, but that's not routine for us.

To illustrate how this point system works take, for example, Mrs. Smith. If she teaches Sunday school, she gets three points. If she serves on the hanging of the greens committee, that's one more point. If she also serves in a women's missionary circle, she gets three more points and is then maxed out. If she is well-qualified, suited, and eager to do activity "A," then we might need to say to her, "If you do 'A,' then we need to let someone else do 'C'" (something she is currently doing).

I serve in a congregation where some people just cannot say no. If I ask them to do something, they'll do it. They may not do everything well, but they agree to help because they don't know how to say no. The point system enables us to help them manage their number of commitments.

Electing the Candidates

+ + + + + + +

Our nominating committee begins its serious work around March 1. Our staff works with this six-member committee to secure our five major program directors. Once we've recruited those leaders, the directors start enlisting their lieutenants. That happens by the end of March. Next, these teams start enlisting workers. Last year we had *about 95 percent of our workers enlisted by May 31*. All of our new workers are ready to take over September 1.

The nominating committee has several tiers or levels under which all of our programs are grouped. We systematically enlist people from level one first, then level two, and then level three. A person serving on a committee is usually in level four, five, or six. The people in leadership—lead teachers or directors, for instance—are farther up in the levels. We staff the positions by filling the heavier responsibilities first.

The nominating committee has a complete printout of everybody who is on the church roll, irrespective of how long they have been attending. As they review and update that listing annually, they keep track of where people are serving. The process works this way: If I recruit someone to teach a class, the nominating committee approves that person, prepares a report, presents it to the church at our annual business meeting, and that person is elected to serve in that position for the next year. At the end of the committee's work, a complete ballot listing all of the people being nominated to serve during the next year is printed and passed out to our church membership. The church members then have the opportunity to approve the nominations at our annual business meeting.

Even though we hope that everybody in our church will serve in some position, with about 1,500 members and only 500 to 600 volunteers, obviously not everybody is serving. However, we are close because out of the 1,500 members, we have around 1,000 whom I would consider active members and 300 to 400 of them are children and youth.

A number of other positions in the church are not elected at the business meeting. We have people who serve as Sunday school class presidents and officers, outreach leaders, prayer chairmen, and so on. The church does not elect them; they are just determined by the classes themselves. When we start incorporating those volunteers, we reach another group of people. So I think we do have more than 80 percent of our adults actually serving.

Here at Bay Leaf, we have a very mobile society. It's affluent—second homes are popular—so our attendance drops off in the summer. I have a lot of leadership that is away during the summer, but I also have a good reservoir of substitutes for Sunday school in particular. During the summer, our Sunday night, Wednesday night, and weekday programs are discontinued. Many people would say that we are a nine-month church—September 1 through Memorial Day—because our programming in the summer is limited to Sunday morning. We have very little beyond that except for youth and single adult activities. We prefer to simply recognize that there are given seasons of ministry within our annual calendar, and we want to offer quality programs when they are running.

While we say that Sunday night and Wednesday night activities are enlistments for a year, they are technically only for the school year, which helps with recruiting. They start September 1 and end June 1. People are willing to make a weekly commitment that still allows them the freedom of being off for the summer.

A Spiritual Endeavor

+ + + + + + +

I don't think everybody is a born teacher. However, I do believe that most people can serve in a class setting if they have a heart for people, are teachable, and are willing to serve. We want volunteers to view teaching as a spiritual endeavor and to feel the Lord has called them to this. We want people who are open to being used by God. A particular individual may not be the best or most ideal teacher, but a teacher with limited skills and compassion for others will have more impact than someone who is simply an excellent presenter. I would rather have someone who truly loves our children than someone who is just good at teaching lessons.

Prior to being placed on the church ballot for a teaching position, *I will have personally talked with that person before he is voted on by the church.* He will also be given a job description and some curriculum to review. We then give him time to look over the material and pray about the possibility, and then we are back in touch in about a week.

Teachers need to know the particulars of the job. They need to know what is expected of them, how much training is required, and how many other meetings are involved. A Sunday school worker does not just come at 9:30 on Sunday morning and finish at 10:45. The job entails much more than an hour or two on Sundays. We have visitors at our church every week, and we expect our children's Sunday school workers to *follow up with visitors*. We expect teachers to go to training opportunities, including departmental meetings. These team meetings are inspirational, motivational, and developmental. Teachers know that all of these expectations are part of the job because we give them a *written job description.*

Currently we do not utilize a spiritual gifts inventory. My experience has been that as people move through those inventories, they either come out with "I'm a teacher" or "I'm not a teacher." When they do that, someone may think, "My gift is not teaching, so therefore, I can't ever stand in front of a group and do any type of presentation." But if that individual has a heart of compassion, we can help that person develop some teaching skills.

Because of the growth at Bay Leaf, we add new classes each year. Thus I am always looking for lead teachers. Our lead teachers usually come out of the worker category—those who are helping somebody else. Part of my role as a pastor is to look for ways to *deepen people in ministry service*. When I see someone helping with crafts in Vacation Bible School or something like that, I start thinking, "What else could she do? Would she work well teaching the first grade, or maybe the third grade?" If I decide that she could work in another position,

I'll contact her. She may say, "Well, I've never taught before." I tell her that the lack of experience is unimportant to me. If she is willing to try, I will help her become comfortable teaching. I will put her into places where she can substitute or team teach and build a little confidence without having the full responsibility.

Success Is Good; Failure Is Okay

+ + + + + +

In our church, it is all right to fail. It is okay for programs to fail. Everything can't be successful. Nevertheless, I don't want an individual in one of our programs to have a bad experience. Each of our volunteers should always feel encouraged. This is why we don't just dump somebody into a ministry vacancy.

I prefer to place people with others to minimize misplacement. For example, I might ask, "Would you assume the responsibility of serving on the hanging of the greens committee?" even though I may have several other people who are already on that committee. Since one person is not going to make or break a particular committee, she can try the service opportunity to check out her "fit" with that position.

This approach is a little more risky when a volunteer is asked to serve in a missions class or Sunday school class where there are only two or three workers. Every person on that team is critical. But since we use lead teachers and assistant teachers in each class, we can still minimize the risk factor for new workers.

I want people to be successful. I want them to feel good about what they are doing. I don't want them to drop out. Yet I still have people who say, "I think the Lord is calling me to teach youth." Then, after a few months, they realize that this is not what they want to do and are ready to get out of it. That's okay with me. Someone's ministry niche is frequently discovered by trying several areas.

If a volunteer senses a need for redirection, I might say, "If this did not work, would you rather go down to the fourth grade or would you feel more comfortable with the college age group?" If the volunteer feels led to teach, I think it is part of my responsibility as minister of education to place him in a position where he can be a successful leader.

Again, since we use a team-teaching approach, our volunteers feel more supported. It is less threatening because all of the responsibility does not fall on one individual. Responsibility is on the group. The team approach works especially well at our church because we are right outside the research triangle where companies such as IBM and Northern Telecom use teams as standard operating procedure. Since our members are used to working that way in business, they are comfortable with it in the church setting as well. One of the other benefits of the team approach is that having two or three workers in a department allows one of them to be away for a Sunday if necessary.

Working Toward Balance

+ + + + + + +

We currently use one-year contracts only for more time-consuming ministry assignments. Some short-term tasks, such as one-point committee assignments, are now on a three-year appointment. People serve for three years, thus we only need to elect a third of those committees every year. But three-point ministries, like teaching, are still appointed annually.

Since our desire is to move people from pew sitters to servants, our leadership looks for a *wide variety of ministry options* for people. Our hospitality committee, for example, not only organizes social times for the congregation—cookies and punch-type things—but also provides coffee and donuts on the first Sunday of every month, and organizes the annual Pig Pickin'—a dinner we have—a Valentine's banquet, and a Sunday school breakfast in October. We also have several Sunday night fellowships scattered throughout the church calendar that they are responsible for organizing.

Originally one committee covered all the social activities for the church. Now we have three subcommittees that oversee these events. The fellowship committee consists of about twenty-five volunteers, the first-Sunday coffee committee has eight volunteers, and the hospitality committee (a new subgroup using the old name) utilizes another twenty-five workers. Because we are moving toward more project-oriented committees, people are willing to give a limited amount of their time. They say, "I'll work on that, but when it's over, that's it."

Our heart's desire at Bay Leaf is to grow people into Christlikeness, and this requires all of the members of the body to "build up one another." We try to distribute the ministry load of the church across the shoulders of the entire congregation. And by using our point system, we try to make sure that our volunteers have times when they come to church as participants. Volunteers give, but they must receive as well. We believe this provides a good balance.

+ + + + + + +

If there's a word to describe Bay Leaf Baptist Church's approach to recruitment, it is systemic. Bay Leaf has developed a system for volunteerism that permeates the entire congregation. Their multiple-committee structure is similar to high-efficiency work teams in the corporate world. Over three dozen task groups carry on the congregation's ministry, and the invitations to volunteer are spread among these committees.

Bay Leaf's system for volunteerism encourages everyone to be involved, yet not overextended. Their decentralized approach reaches deep into the congregation with multiple committee leaders soliciting involvement. At the same time, their point system protects people from exhaustion in their service. By including the names of teachers on their annual May ballot, Bay Leaf's system for volunteerism assures advanced enlistment and the possibility for early preparation for service.

Finding enough volunteers to run a fine Christian education program is always a challenge. Spreading the responsibility across a team of shoulders only makes sense. Bay Leaf's systemic approach to volunteerism will interest a growing number of congregations.

Ministry Resources

The following materials are used at Bay Leaf Baptist Church in their Christian education ministries. Permission to use and adapt these resources in your congregation is granted. Duplication or distribution of these copyrighted materials for resale is prohibited.

BAY LEAF'S VOLUNTEER POINT SYSTEM

OBJECTIVE: Every member of the church will utilize his gifts and abilities in service through his local church.

CONCEPT: All volunteer positions in the church will be given a numerical value in order to evaluate whether a few church members are doing too much of the work load.

PURPOSE: Utilizing this concept will assist us in preventing burnout for some members, but will also force us to look for a large volunteer base from which to provide for the ministries of our church.

PROCESS:

3-point positions:	**2-point positions:**	**1-point positions:**
These positions require regular teaching preparation for weekly meetings.	These positions require regular preparation for monthly or weekly meetings.	These positions are for committees that require only short-term preparation.
Deacon	Adult choir member	Most church committees
Sunday school teacher	Music ensemble leaders and members	
Mission organization leaders	Major committees: personnel, stewardship, etc.	
Bible study leaders		

IDEAL: No one should have more than seven points.

BOTTOM LINE: More people enjoy serving in volunteer positions and fewer people are overloaded with an undue work load.

BAY LEAF BAPTIST CHURCH'S
MINISTRIES SURVEY

NAME _____ DATE _____

OCCUPATION _____ PHONE _____

(Information given will be used by the ministerial staff, the nominating committee, and church program leaders to ascertain members' interests, gifts, and abilities, and enable members to find significant and fulfilling ways in which to express love for and faith in God through service and ministry to our church family and local community.)

PART I—CHURCH PROGRAM ORGANIZATIONS
(Please check the appropriate space and fill in the blanks.)

	Past Experience	Now Serving	Would Consider	P-Preach C-Children Y-Youth A-Adult		Past Experience	Now Serving	Would Consider
SUNDAY SCHOOL					**MISSION ORGANIZATIONS**			
Department Director					WMU Director			
Teacher					Baptist Women Officer			
Asst. or Sub. Teacher					Women's Circle Leader			
Secretary					Acteens Ldr (Gr 6-12)			
Outreach Care Leader					G.A. Leader (Gr 1-5)			
Vacation Bible School					Mission Friends Leader			
General Officer					Baptist Men's Leader			
					R. A. Leader (Gr 1-5)			
DISCIPLESHIP TRAINING					R. A. Leader (Gr 6-12)			
Group Leader					**MUSIC MINISTRY**			
Leadership Training					Preschool Choir Leader			
Special Projects					Preschool Choir Helper			
Bible Study Leader					Children's Choir Leader			
Precept Leader					Children's Choir Helper			
Children's Bible Drill					Youth Choir Leader			
					Adult Choir Member			
PASTORAL CARE					Handbell Choir Member			
Deacon					Play Piano/Organ			
Ordained Minister					Play Other Instruments			
Care Ministry					Music Librarian			

(continued)

MINISTRIES SURVEY—PART II—CHURCH COMMITTEES

COMMITTEES	Past Experience	Now Serving	Would Consider	COMMITTEES	Past Experience	Now Serving	Would Consider
Activities				Interior Design			
Advisory				Kitchen			
Audiovisual				Library			
Baptism				Long-Range Planning			
Bereavement				Maintenance—Building			
Care				Maintenance—Grounds			
Cemetery				Missions			
Children's Activity				Music			
Children's Worship				New Member			
Clothes Closet				Nominating			
Communion				Personnel			
Computer				Publicity			
Constitution				Senior Citizens			
Flower				Stewardship			
Greeters				Transportation			
Homebound				Trustees			
Homecoming				Ushering			
Hospitality				Youth			

PART III—SPECIALIZED MINISTRIES/TALENTS

RECREATIONAL MINISTRIES	Past Experience	Now Serving	Would Consider		Past Experience	Now Serving	Would Consider
Softball				Golf			
Exercise Program				Basketball			
Tennis				Coach or Official			
				Other _____			

(continued)

	Past Experience	Now Serving	Would Consider		Past Experience	Now Serving	Would Consider
MINISTRIES/ TALENTS				MINISTRIES/ TALENTS			
Clothing Closet				Secretarial Assistance			
Crafts				Sewing			
Deliver Meals				Angel Tree			
Decorating				Visitation			
Carpentry Work				Messengers to			
Lights, Props, Staging				Baptist Conventions			
Projector, Slide,				Costumes			
Video Operator				Mission Projects			
First Aid, Rescue, CPR				Prayer Chain			
Gardening/Yard Care				and Ministries			
Ministry to Elderly/				Drama			
Homebound				Child Care During			
Photography				Worship			
Posters/Bulletin Boards				Bus/Van Driver			
Puppets							

*( ) I would consider working in the area(s) checked above, but will need training.

Please return to the church office.

RESPONSIBILITIES OF CHILDREN'S SUNDAY SCHOOL TEACHERS

Responsibilities of a teacher are to

1. **Guide** children to know God and His redemptive message in the Bible. Lead girls and boys to accept Christ when they are so convicted by the Holy Spirit.
   - Guide a group of children in Bible study giving guidance to individual Bible study activities.
   - Assist the department director in Bible study activities and fellowship activities.
   - Be able to counsel children concerning God and His redemptive plan.

2. **Promote,** encourage, and participate in In-reach, Home-reach, and Outreach activities, including evangelistic visitation and ministry.
   - Visit or contact absentees each week.
   - Provide current information to the department director concerning prayer concerns and needs.

3. **Cooperate** with other children's workers in discovering and cultivating prospects and their families and in cultivating members and their families.
   - Assist with maintaining an up-to-date department prospect file.
   - Encourage and participate in weekly evangelistic visitation efforts.

4. **Participate** in regularly scheduled weekly or monthly workers meetings.
   - Be prepared for weekly or monthly workers meetings by studying the unit Bible material and suggested teaching procedures.
   - Encourage other workers to participate in weekly or monthly workers meetings.

5. **Engage** in training and study activities to improve effectiveness in teaching, reaching, and evangelistic witnessing.
   - Assist department director in planning, doing, and evaluating the work of the department through use of the *Children's Sunday School Standard*.

6. **Attend** and support church worship services and the church programs and emphases.
   - Assist the department director in cooperating with other children's programs in the use of children's space, equipment, and materials used for Sunday School.
   - Attend worship services regularly.

NOMINATING COMMITTEE REPORT

Church Officers, Church Program Leadership, and Committees, 1997-1998

I. CHURCH OFFICERS

AUDITOR	CHURCH CLERK	TREASURER	TRUSTEES
Paul Casey	Wendy Lassiter	Bill Schneider	Bill Nipper (C) (1)
			Tom Hardee (2)
			Bob Hughes (3)

II. CHURCH PROGRAMS
SUNDAY SCHOOL

Director: Ron Kellam
Asst. Director—Literature and Supplies: Marshall Simmons
Asst. Director—Registration/Greeter: Walt Haskins
Sunday School Secretary: Ruebelle Strickland

PRESCHOOL DIVISION

Sunday School Director
Shelly Kangas

Sunday School Asst. Director

Preschool I (Babies)
Sandy Auler
Kathy Freeman
Jim Loehman
Glenda Loehman
Jenny Kmak
Lola Bailey
Sally Weber
Angie King

Preschool II (Younger 1's) 1A
Jane Bailey
Susan Harris
Brenda Hunsinger

Preschool III (Older 1's) 1B
Renee Riggs
Deanne Grice
Melissa Scott

Preschool IV (Younger 2's)
Sherry Wallace
Rebecca Carter

Preschool V (Older 2's)
Linda Simmons
Judy Wilkinson

Preschool VI (3's) 3A
Pat Paschall
Kathy Brown
Christy Wisemen

Preschool VII (4's) 4A
Pam and Jim McNeill

Preschool VIII (4's) 4B
Cindy Finger
Denise Capley

Preschool IX (A) (5's) 5A
Will and Kathy Warren
Beverly Sherman

Preschool X (B) Kindergarten 5B
Steve Scott
Stephanie Vanderhyde
Heidi Southworth

CHILDREN'S DIVISION

Director
Pat Peterson

Children I (Grade 1A)
Jane Osborne

Children II (Grade 1B)
Martha King
Deanna Brown

Children II (Grade 2A)
Trisha Duckett
Paula Lassiter

Children III (Grade 2B)
Colleen Remein
Ann Casey

Children IV (Grade 3)
Ann Wofford
Nancy Ports

Children V (Grade 4A)
Wanda Mandeville

Children VI (Grade 4B)
Keith Whitley

Children VII (Grade 5)
Ron and Barbara Neill

EDITOR'S NOTE: The actual report is much lengthier. This is an example of one page from that report.

Chapter Four

Vote for Kids: A Thematic Approach

**Grace Church
Edina, Minnesota**

Your family just moved to the south side of Minneapolis and, because of its reputation, you're encouraged to visit Grace Church of Edina. As you pull off France Avenue, you struggle to locate a parking space. But once inside, the information booth is easy to spot. A warm receptionist guides you and your children to their classes. Hallways are crowded as the second of four worship services is about to begin. Then, standing above the crowd, is an eight-foot character who appears to be Uncle Sam. He greets your children; they giggle. He hands them each a button and says, "Vote for Kids."

Vote for Kids was one of the annual themes used by the children's department at Grace Church. Since God loves children, and since it was an election year, children's pastor Walt Pitman chose that theme to promote the children's work among the congregation. In fact, Walt himself played the character of Uncle Sam. "SAM" is an acronym for "Share A Ministry." The hallways were all decked out with red, white, and blue flyers stressing the importance of children's ministry. Walt Pitman tells us more about this thematic approach to recruitment and their Christian education ministry.

Our Philosophy

+ + + + + + +

When we promote the needs of our children's ministry, we want to have a positive image among our congregation. I've come to the conclusion that the majority of people want to be part of something that is positive. People respond to something that is significant, something that will make an impact on their lives.

For this reason, each year we center our recruitment efforts around a theme. I don't feel a theme is something disposable that we use for just two weeks or a month. At Grace Church, we choose a theme as a yearlong approach to our children's ministry. In the "Vote for Kids" theme, for example, we decorated specific places in the church with red, white, and blue bunting, Olympic symbols, and "Vote for Kids" posters. The teaching staff wore red, white, and blue buttons that announced, "Vote for Kids." The children wore buttons, affirming the importance of ministry among them. But the theme was not used just to get new volunteers. Rather, it was used throughout the year to highlight the importance of ministry to children. Whether it was special events, teachers meetings, or the annual appreciation banquet, our job that year was to "Vote for Kids" through our own faithful service.

The previous year we used the theme "Big Steps, Little Feet" to promote the importance of adults leading children. Playing off a song by Mary Rice-Hopkins, we highlighted the significance of walking and working with children. Next, we plan to use the theme "Kid's Express" with a locomotive as our logo and a stationmaster as our point person. The annual themes help our congregation recognize the precious commodity that we have in our children. They invite them to participate in the life-transforming adventure of teaching. An annual theme raises awareness and captivates interest.

Ministry Begins With Attitude

+ + + + + + +

How are we going to present our children's ministry to the congregation? Are we going to present it in a negative, problem-focused way? Or are we going to promote it as a thing of beauty and value? How people think leads to what they decide.

Let me use an analogy. Imagine that you want to go on a cruise. As you approach the dock, you see two ships anchored. The first is an old, trashy-looking freighter. It hasn't been painted; there is rust all over it. But on the other side of the pier is a luxury liner, let's say the QE II. Which ship would you rather climb aboard?

When it comes to ministry, some programs present themselves in woeful disrepair. Inadequate classrooms beckon for new teachers; desperate ministers use guilt to enlist a crew. Other programs, just as much in need of workers, present the positive features and values of the ship. Service on the second ship is much more inviting.

I have chosen to present our children's ministry as the QE II. At Grace, *we have chosen to present a positive image*. Instead of pleading to the congregation, "We need two hundred more workers," our focus is "Thank you for the four hundred who have already volunteered to serve. There are still ministry opportunities for two hundred more people."

The need hasn't changed, but it is presented in a positive way that honors God. People are more likely to want to jump on the ship that's presented in the most attractive way. When we recruit in a positive manner, people want to come aboard.

I am persuaded that it is not difficult to recruit people if you're willing to use any warm body. The challenge is to *recruit people with integrity*. That means involving people who want to be there, who want to serve God and serve children. That's why recruitment approaches need to reflect a positive image as opposed to a negative or guilt-ridden image.

Guilt works, of course. It influences people. In churches across America, one of the reasons guilt is used as a motivator is that it works in the short term. But in the long term, I think it is devastating. We must look at recruitment for the long term. Today I may get volunteers through guilt, but I'll also experience a high rate of turnover because these people are not happy being there. If they've had their arms twisted, they are not going to want to serve again. Over the long haul, it is more beneficial to present a positive image of what we are doing so that people will want to be a part of it.

Attitude is important. Unfortunately, some people shortsightedly believe that working with children isn't very important. Some refer to events in the nursery or the two-year-old class or even working with five-year-olds as "baby-sitting." I've even heard professionally paid staff refer to their nursery ministry as baby-sitting or to early childhood ministries as child care. They speak of it almost as if it is simply child care on Sunday mornings. By implication they are saying that nothing spiritual is going on there, that these volunteers are just taking care of the kids so that the "real" ministry with adults can take place elsewhere.

When that kind of attitude is verbalized to people, a feeling is established that children's ministry is not important. I have no hesitation about correcting that attitude. Even if a senior pastor lets that attitude slip out, let's say at a staff meeting, I have no problem stopping and interjecting, "Remember, we don't do child care, we don't do baby-sitting; we do ministry with children." *I want everyone to value children's ministry.* Our terminology about our work with children is important! We need to use service terminology in children's ministry in order to help people understand that working with children is not only important, but a vital way to grow our church.

Positive speech about children's ministry must begin among the teaching staff if it's to be caught by the larger congregation. We are all recruiters for children's ministry! The only question is whether what we say encourages or discourages people from volunteering. In our training, I help people understand that what we say about children's ministry dictates people's receptivity to being a part of that ministry. If people communicate that their job is a terrible assignment but because of a commitment to God they are there, those folks are going to be there by themselves for a long time.

Instead, we communicate in a positive way: "I had a great time on Sunday. We had a lot of kids for the number of teachers, but I know that what I am doing is making a difference in a child's life. It is significant. It is meaningful. I live for those kids coming up to me and giving me hugs every Sunday."

When we do that, then all of a sudden people start to say, "Wait a minute. John over there is doing something significant with his life. He is touching lives and enjoying it. He is part of a team. I'd like to do that! Tell me more. How can I get involved?"

At that point we are able to tell them what the responsibilities of a table teacher are, for example. Then we can add, "If I can do it, you can do it."

Whether in the office, in a small group, in the hallway at church, or on the golf course, people should catch a positive view of children's ministry from us. Presenting a positive image is expressed not just in print. It is not limited to what is said from the pulpit. It is also those *positive comments that we make to one another that carry the most weight.* I think that is very important. The willingness of people to be open to service largely depends on how positive our teachers and parents are about their experience. Growing Christians all want to be part of a significant ministry.

The Priority of Children

+ + + + + + +

When we begin to plan a recruitment campaign, it always comes back to why we do what we do. When people ask me about recruitment, for example, I usually reply with the question, "What is it that you're trying to accomplish? What are your goals for this ministry? What is your mission statement? What is your philosophy of ministry?" The answers to these questions will dictate how a church goes about its ongoing ministry and inviting volunteers to serve.

The church whose purpose is to minister primarily to adults will run a children's ministry in a distinctly different way than a church where the focus is on all individuals, including children.

As we work with families in our church, one of the basic questions we ask is, "Why do we have a children's ministry?" The answer to this question dictates how recruitment is handled. So I may ask myself, "Is this a ministry for children? Or is this a ministry for the parents dropping off the children? Which is it? Or is it both?" At Grace Church, our first priority in children's ministry is our boys and girls. We want to see children grow in their faith. We have an extensive mission statement, but the basic idea is that boys and girls are our primary priority.

With that underlying philosophy, we can then make programmatic decisions. Our recruitment procedures are guided by what is best for boys and girls. Again, this is different than asking what is best for the parent or the volunteer. In other words, what are our priorities? Who is going to be most important in our decision-making process? We have identified the children as our highest priority.

With children being first, we believe that the second most important person is the children's worker, many of whom are parents. They also happen to be the people I deal with the most.

Third in importance, certainly, are the parents. In our ministry to boys and girls, we are not only serving the children, but we are also supporting and helping our parents. While programs are going on for adults, we are simultaneously ministering to children. They are tied together. These three levels of importance help us to establish priorities in decision making, not to indicate worth.

Now someone might say, "OK, that's simple. What children's ministry isn't going to agree with that?" Although I haven't found anybody who disagrees with it, I have found a lot of people who demonstrate that they disagree with it by how they organize their children's ministry. We see it in churches that tend to come up with "creative" alternatives for volunteer staffing. They may go to an every-other-week kind of a format. They may have three teams that alternate in and out of the classroom throughout the year. There are all kinds of other strategies, for example, a teacher serving once a month, one month on, two months off.

A lot of times these churches are recruiting on a rotation basis because they have run out of options. That may be all they can do. But I want to ask, "What is best for the child? Is it going to be best for the child to have a different worker every week?" The answer to that is no. But if I ask, "Do workers want to do it that way?" too often the answer is yes. Every church has truly committed people who want to be in the ministry and who want to be able to teach children week after week. These are the volunteers who give it their all. No church has enough of those people. Unfortunately, many people in our churches do not want to commit to weekly classroom responsibility.

Avoiding the Inoculation Trap

✝ ✝ ✝ ✝ ✝ ✝ ✝

Our philosophy, therefore, influences the procedural decisions that we make. For example, decisions about alternative forms of recruiting, such as once-a-month rotations, are not consistent with our goals, and therefore are not our first approach. Rotational staffing is not consistent with placing children as our top priority.

There are other ramifications to these decisions. The place where these other forms of staffing seem to happen most is in the nursery. A lot of times in early childhood ministry, churches use rotating teams. More often than not, it is a once-a-month type of a worker.

The first thing that happens in this type of situation is that it multiplies fourfold or greater the number of workers needed for that ongoing ministry. Then the obvious question is, "Do we have enough manpower to be able to accomplish that?" In the vast majority of churches, the answer is no. But for me there is a more basic philosophical concern. Volunteer approaches that use periodic service can inoculate people against ministry. They will accept only a limited commitment to ministry. That becomes a trap.

The reason I say that is once-a-month workers forget 25 percent of the time or more that this is their time of the month to serve. Too many are inconsistent. This greatly contributes to the turnover of nursery directors because they are constantly trying to recruit. They see too many uncommitted people who neglect their responsibility, and the directors get burned out.

In the classroom where teachers serve on a once-a-month basis, the children are not nearly as familiar with the workers. And when children are not familiar with the workers, it creates insecurity in their life and the children act out by misbehaving, which requires more care and discipline. In the nursery, the babies are going to cry more, which is not a pleasant experience for the children or the adults.

When a child gets a little bit older—perhaps four or five—and that rotation happens, he is old enough to start expressing his discomfort more clearly and doing what he can to resist going into his classroom. Volunteers who are not there every week become frustrated with the discipline problems in their classrooms. The kids say they don't like Sunday school, and the volunteers don't return next year. This type of children's ministry is organized for conflict because the philosophy says one thing, but the organization says something else.

High-Value Service

+ + + + + + +

If all we are doing is baby-sitting, why don't we just hire people to do that? But if we want to get somebody involved in ministry, then we need to *communicate to volunteers that what they are doing is significant*. We tell them that right where they are serving, they are doing ministry. They are ministers. They are not doing this so that ministry can take place someplace else on the campus. They are doing real ministry right there—in the nursery, in the classroom, in the midweek club.

There are other practical issues that are part of placing a high value on children's ministry, such as how many teachers should be in a classroom. Teacher-to-student ratios are important. In our ministry, we have identified our target teacher-student ratio for each age level. We have identified the classroom size and how many square feet we want to have per child. We have compared what the ideal department size should be with the actual department size. And we have put together this objective criteria to let us know whether or not we are accomplishing our goals. *Adequate staff and space all contribute to volunteer retention.*

I don't know that we are ever going to be at 100 percent with all of these criteria. We certainly are not meeting them now. We have far more kids than we have space for them. In a congregation that has six services and four learning hours, the space issue is always a challenge. Still, it is my job to make the best assignments possible, so I am always going over our goals and resources.

Each fall we promote our children to their new classes. Basically, we are moving children from one room to another, based on the number of children and teachers now needed. None of us would feel good with a one-to-six ratio in the nursery, nor could we afford a one-to-one ratio. So our leadership team makes the necessary assignments and subsequent adjustments to guarantee a secure and sound learning experience for all of our children. This is our challenge.

Though Grace Church needs hundreds of workers each year, any warm body won't do. Once these workers are recruited and have signed on the dotted line, much happens throughout the year by way of encouragement and training to make the theme a reality. Grace Church, in fact, does "Vote for Kids" and affirms their children throughout the year.

For most of us, life in the twenty-first century is busy. Most people have more on their to-do list than they can possibly accomplish. Yet sincere Christians want to serve their Lord. They want to use their time and spiritual gifts wisely. Therefore, a program perceived as valuable is worth being in. A catchy, visible theme captures attention. One church, for example, using the theme "Feed My Sheep," had each child wear a badge with a picture of a lamb on it. Teachers wore badges that said, "I feed sheep." The posters and announcements during their recruitment campaign invited others to join them by stating, "You can feed sheep too!"

A challenging theme must first be based on, and consistent with, a well-thought-out biblical philosophy of ministry. Grace Church has found that they can use this integrated approach as a rallying point at the beginning of the year for recruitment, and as a theme for esprit de corps during the year for teachers and the celebration at the end of the year for a successful term of service. Likewise, other churches have also found that an annual theme can raise the awareness and status of the educational ministry within their congregations.

Ministry Resources

The following materials are used at Grace Church of Edina in their Christian education ministries. Permission to use and adapt these resources in your congregation is granted. Duplication or distribution of these copyrighted materials for resale is prohibited.

VOLUNTEER STAFF APPLICATION

DIRECTORY INFORMATION

Last Name _____ First Name _____ Birthday __/__/__

Street _____ City _____ Zip _____

Home Phone _____ Work Phone _____ E-mail _____

FAMILY

Marital Status _____ Spouse's Name _____ Anniversary __/__/__

Children: Name _____ Age _____ Name _____ Age _____

Name _____ Age _____ Name _____ Age _____

EDUCATION/EMPLOYMENT

Current Employer _____ Phone _____ OK to Call? ❏ yes ❏ no

Job Title or Description _____

List schools attended (post-high school only)

Name of   Dates   Date of
School _____ attended _____ Degree _____ Graduation __/__/__

Name of   Dates   Date of
School _____ attended _____ Degree _____ Graduation __/__/__

GRACE CHURCH ATTENDANCE

Member of Grace Church? ❏ yes ❏ no   Number of years attended _____

Where did you previously attend? _____

How long? _____ Small church you attend? _____

Do you agree with the Grace Church Statement of Faith? ❏ yes ❏ no

CURRENT WALK WITH THE LORD

Year you became a Christian _____

Please summarize your testimony:

(continued)

Is there any area in your life that you would like to change to make yourself a better example to children?

Have you ever   Have you ever   Are you presently being
discipled anyone? _____   been discipled? _____   held accountable? _____   By whom? _____

What are your spiritual goals and dreams?

What do you like best about working with children?

What are your hobbies, special abilities?

What are your spiritual gifts?

As a leader, what is your standard in the following areas: drugs, alcohol, tobacco?

MINISTRY EXPERIENCE, CURRENT AND PAST

Ministry _____   Ministry_____

When _____   When _____

Where _____   Where _____

Person you reported to _____   Person you reported to _____

Phone _____   Phone _____

(continued)

SELF-DESCRIPTION

Please circle every word or phrase that best describes a consistent character trait of yours. Circle as many as describe you.

L. Takes charge, Assertive, Bold, Enterprising, Decision maker, Goal-driven, Enjoys challenges, Determined, Firm, Purposeful, Competitive, Leader, Self-reliant, Adventurous, "Let's do it now."

O. Takes risks, Motivator, Fun-loving, Very verbal, Enjoys change, Group-oriented, Avoids detail, Visionary, Energetic, Likes variety, Promoter, Creative, Mixes easily, Optimistic, "Trust me, it will work out."

G. Loyal, Even keeled, Enjoys routine, Good listener, Sympathetic, Nurturing, Tolerant, Nondemanding, Avoids conflict, Dislikes change, Adaptable, Thoughtful, Patient, Deep relationships, "Let's keep things the way they are."

B. Deliberate, Reserved, Practical, Factual, Detailed, Inquisitive, Persistent, Controlled, Predictable, Orderly, Discerning, Analytical, Precise, Scheduled, "How was it done in the past?"

REFERENCES

Please provide two Grace Church character references who can identify your strengths and weaknesses.

Name _____ Phone _____

Name _____ Phone _____

MY COVENANT

TO CHRIST AND THE CHURCH: I believe in the ministry of Grace Church. With God's help, I will be involved and faithful in my assigned ministry, attend meetings and training sessions unless providentially hindered, follow the leadership of my area, and seek to live a consistent life as a Christian. I willingly and joyfully commit myself to the ministry of the church for the glory of Jesus Christ.

Have you ever been accused, rightly or wrongly, of child abuse, sexual abuse, or sexual misconduct?

❏ yes ❏ no

Have you been arrested for or convicted of any criminal act more serious than a traffic violation?

❏ yes ❏ no

I, the undersigned, give my authorization to Grace Church to verify the information on this form. Grace Church may contact my references and appropriate government agencies as deemed necessary in order to verify my suitability as a volunteer staff person.

Signature _____ Date _____

CHILDREN'S MINISTRIES RESPONSE FORM

Date _____ Class _____

Children's Ministries

Promotion Sunday

Children's Ministry Basic Training
September 20 & 21
Friday 6:30 - 9:00 P.M., North Hall (*Dinner Included*)
Saturday 9:00 A.M. - 12:30 P.M., North Hall

Yes, I am interested in learning about children's ministry! Please contact me with more information.

Name _____ Youth/Adult

Address _____ City _____ Zip _____

Day Phone _____ Evening Phone _____ E-mail _____

Area I am most interested in:
❑ Babies/Toddlers   ❑ Ages 2-5   ❑ Grades 1-6   ❑ Awana   ❑ Sports Plus
❑ Puppet/Drama Team   ❑ Missions Education   ❑ Office/Computer   ❑ Graphic Artist   ❑ Other _____

Yes, I am interested in learning about children's ministry! Please contact me with more information.

Name _____ Youth/Adult

Address _____ City _____ Zip _____

Day Phone _____ Evening Phone _____ E-mail _____

Area I am most interested in:
❑ Babies/Toddlers   ❑ Ages 2-5   ❑ Grades 1-6   ❑ Awana   ❑ Sports Plus
❑ Puppet/Drama Team   ❑ Missions Education   ❑ Office/Computer   ❑ Graphic Artist   ❑ Other _____

Yes, I am interested in learning about children's ministry! Please contact me with more information.

Name _____ Youth/Adult

Address _____ City _____ Zip _____

Day Phone _____ Evening Phone _____ E-mail _____

Area I am most interested in:
❑ Babies/Toddlers   ❑ Ages 2-5   ❑ Grades 1-6   ❑ Awana   ❑ Sports Plus
❑ Puppet/Drama Team   ❑ Missions Education   ❑ Office/Computer   ❑ Graphic Artist   ❑ Other _____

PASTORAL PROMOTION OF CHILDREN'S MINISTRIES

A Word from the Pastor

As a church family, our first priority is the nurturing and developing of our children. I encourage you to prayerfully consider being part of the children's team this fall. I am confident that your life will be blessed. Your "flock" of children will grow in God's love and grace through you.

And we, as a church family, will be faithful to both our kids and to the Lord. Pastor Walt will provide excellent training. You'll be working with a team of other adults. And your kids will love you for it!

Please respond by calling the children's office at 924-4270. Our kids need you and they need you *now*. Thanks, dear friend, for responding. God bless you wonderfully in these opportune days of ministry!

Pastor Eagen

Children's Sunday Morning Staffing Needs
Two Views

By Ministry	Total Needed	Committed	Still Needed	% Committed
Nursery	326	226	100	69%
Early Childhood	208	35	173	17%
Grade School	99	39	60	39%
Sun. AM Need	633	300	333	47%

By Hour	Total Needed	Committed	Still Needed	% Committed
8:30	126	82	44	65%
9:50	266	139	127	52%
11:15	124	45	79	36%

CHILDREN'S MINISTRY
GRACE ★ CHURCH

5300 France Avenue S., Edina, MN 55410 (612) 924-4270

*"Train up a child in the way he should go,
even when he is old he will not depart from it."*
—Proverbs 22:6

We welcome you and your children to Grace Church Edina. Children are important people at GCE and we are dedicated to partnering with you in the cultivation of spiritual growth of your children. Our mission in serving you is to provide the best possible care, comfort, guidance, and instruction in the Word of God for your children and their leaders. The Bible is our curriculum . . . printed materials and programs are our resources . . . and adult volunteers are our living examples demonstrating the love of God and life-changing principles to your child. Our goal is that children be loved, valued, and nurtured in their faith! At Grace Church Edina, we want only the best for our children!

AGE-APPROPRIATE!

- **Nursery Ministries**—For the first two+ years of life, we focus on making a child's and parent's initial experience at church a positive and safe one! We want children to learn God's love at the earliest opportunity. We begin with lots of hugs for the babies and sharing simple Bible stories and songs about Jesus that toddlers enjoy!

> **"Our goal is that children be loved, valued, and nurtured in their faith!"**

- **Early Childhood Ministries**—For ages two through five, our priority is for the young child to enjoy learning about God and His Bible! We introduce preschoolers to their heavenly Father through His Word, and encourage them to discover God's love in His creation. By the time a child is five years old, he will have learned the basic stories of creation, the Old Testament, and the life of Christ. Through a variety of Bible learning activities, children will learn the truth of God's Word at their level of comprehension.

(continued)

- **Grade-School Ministries**—Our goal for the elementary child, grades 1 through 6, is both to have fun and be spiritually challenged. Through a systematic study of the Word of God, children are encouraged to explore "what God says," "what it means to me," "and how it can be applied to my life." In fact, by the sixth grade, children will have overviewed the entire Bible six times. We strive for a well-rounded ministry of instruction, evangelism, discipleship, Bible memory, outreach events, missions, worship, sports activities, music, special events, and ministry opportunities.

> **"We are committed to ministry with children, not baby-sitting!"**

FUN WITH A PURPOSE

- **Sunday school (Sunday, 9:50 A.M.)** is what we consider to be our foundational hour of Bible instruction for children. It is a time of exciting Bible stories and personal application of God's Word to a child's life. We hope ALL children will be active participants in the time of discovery! A loving, caring teacher will guide your child to learn the tremendous truths about the Bible, God's Word.

- **Church time (Sunday, 8:30 and 11:15 A.M.)** is designed for children to express their faith through worship experiences, music instruction, and life situation case studies. God and the Bible are shown to be relevant for today's child! The curriculum for preschoolers is correlated to the lesson introduced in Sunday school. For more information about children's music, contact the music ministry office.

> **"The key to our children's ministry is our volunteer workers!"**

- **Awana (Wednesday, 6:45 P.M.)** stands for "Approved Workmen Are Not Ashamed." Wednesday evening's fun and games are definitely the highlight of every child's week. Awana has three focuses: Bible memory, outreach to friends, and of course, lots and lots of FUN! Come to the foyer of the gym to register for Awana.

(continued)

- **Vacation Bible School** is our single largest yearly event for children. Over 800 children and adults laugh and play, learn and grow at Vacation Bible School. Each year we enjoy a new action-packed theme, such as "Aslan Is Near," "Treasure Island," "The Wild West Show," "Indiana Smith and the Pearl of Great Price," and "Deep Space 5: The Regeneration." Don't miss the children's ministry highlight of the year. Reserve the middle of July for the adventure of your life!

- **Special Holiday Programs**—camps, summer day camps, backyard clubs, seminars, family film night, and many other activities round out a ministry to children and their families! Do not be surprised if you see "Jellybean" and "Sweet♥Tart" the clown, "Uncle S.A.M." (Sharing A Ministry), "Cubbie Bear," or "Sparkle" greeting children on Saturdays and Sundays at Grace Church Edina. Clowns, puppets, mimes, and jugglers may show up on any weekend and often do so to encourage children to bring friends and grow in their faith. We are committed to strengthening today's families through the Word of God shared creatively and through events designed to promote better family communications!

- **Sound exciting!?** Grace Church Edina children's ministry is one of the most exciting places for children to be! We want children of Grace Church Edina not only to grow spiritually, but also to have fun being a child!

Children are a gift from the Lord (Psalm 127:3), a gift requiring loving care and guidance. Parents are the primary teachers of their children (Deuteronomy 6:6-9). We are here to help you grow a beautiful person by assisting you in cultivating spiritual growth in your child. We encourage you to review weekly take-home papers with your child. Together enjoy the Bible memory work, club projects, and resources available in the library.

We are committed to *ministry with children, not baby-sitting*. Our focus is never on child care, but rather on nurturing children, serving parents, and training leaders. The key to our children's ministry is the volunteer staff who must reflect Christlikeness before the children. It requires over 800 workers each week to reach out to the boys and girls God has brought to us. As you become a regular attender of Grace Church Edina, please consider where you will be involved in the children's ministry!

"Touching Lives and Changing Hearts"

Our Vision for children's ministry at Grace Church Edina is that we are dedicated to *partnering* with parents in cultivating personal spiritual growth with their children.

Our Mission is to provide the best possible care, comfort, guidance, and instruction in the Word of God for children, parents, and their leaders.
- The *Bible* is our curriculum.
- *Printed materials*, *budgets*, and *programs* are our resources, and . . .
- *Adult volunteers* are our living examples demonstrating the love of God and life-changing principles to children.

Our Philosophy can be summarized by the statement, "Come, Grow, and Go." In other words, we are committed to *evangelism*, *discipleship*, and *missions*.

Our Goal is that children be *loved*, *valued*, and *nurtured* in their faith as they become committed followers of Jesus Christ! Children are important people at Grace Church and we want only the best for our children!

Our Objectives: We will know that we are accomplishing our purpose with children as they . . .
1. *Know* that God loves them and sent His Son, Jesus Christ, to be their Savior.
2. Become a member of God's *forever family* by believing in Jesus Christ as their personal Savior and Lord.
3. *Grow* as a Christian, developing a lifestyle that is pleasing to God and showing others that they are committed followers of Jesus Christ.
4. Develop a *personal*, growing relationship with God, seeking His guidance in *prayer* for all life's situations and problems.
5. *Love*, *obey*, and *apply* God's Word by learning skills for personal Bible study and memorization, so that they can *discover* for themselves what the Bible means.
6. Express their love for God through *worship*, *praise*, and *musical presentations*.
7. *Enjoy* the church, Christ's body; develop Christian friendships with members of God's family, both adults and peers.
8. *Identify* their God-given gifts so they can develop and use them for God's glory.
9. *Serve* and *love* others by participating in opportunities to help those in need and share their faith both *locally* and *cross-culturally*.
10. Feel *loved* and valued as *individuals*.

VOLUNTEER WORKER EXPECTATIONS

Worker Qualifications

1. Heart for God!
2. Heart for His Church!
3. Heart for His Children!

What We Expect From Our Volunteer Workers

1. Enjoy what you're doing—Have fun!
2. Tell others that you're enjoying it! (You can be our best or worst recruiter.)
3. Be positive and optimistic!
4. Be on time (15-20 minutes before the scheduled start time)!
5. Be here every week!
6. Be a friend to "your" kids!
7. Be a model and an example to kids!
8. Be a friend to other leaders!
9. Say "I love you" to kids by . . .

    Calling them on the phone.

    Writing them notes and cards.

    Visiting them in their homes.

    Taking them out for a pop or yogurt.

    Smiling and using their names.

10. Attend TEAM nights (our monthly training meetings)!
11. Have an "Oh, boy" attitude!

VOLUNTEER WORKER'S OUTREACH EVALUATION FORM

Making a Difference in Kids' Lives

Finding the Children

In the past three (or six) months, how many new children have visited your class as a result of:

- Planned leader or teacher outreach efforts?
- Invitation by a child in group (or child's parents)?
- Invitation by someone in the church?
- Child's or parents' own initiative?
- Child's participation in other church programs (VBS, club, choir, social, etc.)?
- Other?

Based on these answers, rate your efforts at finding new children:

       1—Excellent   2—Satisfactory   3—Needs Improvement

List the names, addresses, and phone numbers of at least three children who could be prospects for your class. These may be children who have visited your class recently, children in your own neighborhood, children of church families who do not currently attend your class.

1. Name _____ Phone _____
   Address _____
2. Name _____ Phone _____
   Address _____
3. Name _____ Phone _____
   Address _____

Contacting Children

In the past three (or six) months, how many children have you personally contacted by:

Visitors	Regulars	
_____	_____	Talking individually before, during, or after class?
_____	_____	Calling the child on the phone?
_____	_____	Visiting the child in the home?
_____	_____	Sending a personal letter or card?
_____	_____	Inviting the child to your home?
_____	_____	Planning a class party?

(continued)

Based on these answers, rate your personal efforts at contacting children:

       1—Excellent   2—Satisfactory   3—Needs Improvement

How many of the visitors are now attending regularly? _____

How important were your contacts in gaining this attendance? _____

_____

How many of the children who are not now attending might still be gained by further contacts?

_____

Plan your contacts for three months. Set a goal for the number of out-of-class contacts you want to make each month:

Visitors	Regulars	
_____	_____	Visits
_____	_____	Phone Calls
_____	_____	Cards and/or Letters
_____	_____	Other

Contacting Families

In the past three (or six) months, how many parents have you personally contacted by:

Visitors	Regulars	
_____	_____	Talking individually before, during, or after class?
_____	_____	Approaching them at other times around church?
_____	_____	Calling on the phone?
_____	_____	Visiting in the home?
_____	_____	Sending a personal letter or card?
_____	_____	Inviting them to observe the class?
_____	_____	Participating with the family in a social activity?
_____	_____	Other?

Based on these answers, rate your personal efforts at contacting children:

       1—Excellent   2—Satisfactory   3—Needs Improvement

List ideas for getting acquainted with parents of children identified as prospects for your class:

FOLLOW-UP GUIDELINES FOR TEACHERS OF CHILDREN

1. Ask teachers to telephone one or more children in their class—visitors, absentees, or regular members. Children enjoy phone calls. A brief conversation can tell an absent child he was missed, encourage a child for good work last Sunday, or remind a child of a coming event or activity.

2. Suggest that teachers send a short note to each child, thanking him/her for something they have done in class.

3. Encourage teachers to make a point of greeting a visitor's parents on the first Sunday and to tell the parents about one specific experience their child enjoyed during the session. Make an appointment with the parents to briefly explain the program.

4. If a teacher has not made a home visit before, have an experienced teacher go as a partner the first time or two. Suggest taking a student's book and possibly a few snapshots of the child in the classroom.

5. One of the most effective contact plans is for a teacher to invite a couple of children at a time to come to his/her home. This can be done on Sunday afternoon or after school. Children that have been indifferent or difficult may undergo dramatic attitude changes as a result of having a good time with the teacher in a casual setting. The advantage of inviting two children is that they entertain each other and stronger friendships are built. Some teachers make a point of combining one child who attends regularly with one who is new or attends irregularly. (Ask the children ahead of time what they like to eat. Keep it simple and let them help with the preparation.)

6. When teachers have had experience and success contacting class members, visitors, and their families, they feel more confident about contacting prospects.

Chapter Five

Seeing Is Believing: A High-Visibility Approach

Ward Evangelical Presbyterian Church
Livonia, Michigan

Picture yourself seated in the auditorium of Ward Evangelical Presbyterian Church, Livonia, Michigan. Corporate worship is the reason for the morning service. But on this spring Lord's Day, prior to a prayer of dedication for teachers, you are startled by a parade like none you've ever seen before. Long lines of children process through the auditorium. First the preschool children come down the center aisle by classes. They are followed by older preschool children, then young elementary children, and then upper elementary students. Wave after wave of children move down the center aisle, moving left and right and filing out the side doors. Music is playing in the background. You're amazed, perhaps staggered, by the sheer volume of children in this congregation.

The children's walk-through at Ward Church helps the congregation see how large a mission field they have right before them. And the Christian education department uses these visible opportunities to invite people to experience the joy of investing their lives in the lives of others. The Reverend Hal Edmonds, pastor of educational ministries, tells us how Ward Church invites volunteers to minister.

A Lesson From the School of Hard Knocks

✦ ✦ ✦ ✦ ✦ ✦ ✦

When I first graduated from seminary, I was called to be the minister of education and youth at a church in southern California. When I arrived at this church, I discovered that the pastor whom I thought I would be working with had left. A new pastor had been assigned to the church by the annual conference. By the time I moved from Pennsylvania to southern California, the new senior pastor had been there only three weeks, so he knew as few people as I did. The church secretary handed us a list and said, "These are all of the vacancies that we have to fill in the Christian education area. The first thing you will want to do is fill all of these vacancies because until they are filled, those ministries will not be happening."

A period of time had elapsed from when the previous minister of education had left and I had arrived, so any teachers wanting to make a change had dropped out. So there we were with a lot of vacancies. The secretary gave us a pictorial directory of the church members, walked us through the pages, and told us who some of the likely workers might be. With that the pastor left on a three-week vacation.

I was left alone, not only to fill those places but also to fill the pastor's role while he was away. My number one priority was to preach on Sunday morning, Sunday evening, and Wednesday night. Second, I had to fill all of those vacancies.

I sat down and called all of the likely candidates. I begged, cajoled, and cried. I did all kinds of things. Three weeks later, when the pastor returned from his vacation, I had filled every one of those jobs. He was excited about that and wondered how in the world I had done it.

However, as the weeks and months rolled by, I discovered that I was refilling those same jobs. At that time, I was not wise enough to realize why I had to keep refilling the same positions. Then one day I was reading Oswald Chambers' book, *My Utmost for His Highest*. One of the devotionals had to do with Jesus asking Peter the question, "Do you love me?" Then He said, "Feed my sheep." Chambers made some statements about servants feeding sheep. He made the observation that a need only represents the opportunity for ministry.

God used that experience to show me that simply filling jobs is not what recruitment is all about. Real recruitment is helping people discover the ministries that God has for them and finding their place in the body of believers. That revolutionized the way I approached recruitment. My job is to present needs, to help people understand what the positions are, and to encourage them to pray and seek God's will. In discovering their ministry, they open their lives to fulfilling their work in the body of believers.

When people find this kind of fulfillment, they are no longer just helping out poor old Hal Edmonds by doing a job. They embrace true ministry and fulfill a function in the body of believers that God has given specifically to them. They discover that service is a sacred trust. I have found that when I am able to help people make this discovery, I do not have to keep filling the same jobs over and over again.

That happened many years ago, but it is the foundation of my thinking when it comes to helping people use their spiritual gifts and filling all those vacancies we have in Christian education.

Eleven Fifty and Still Growing

+ + + + + + +

At Ward Church, we have a very broad program. Our leadership team is responsible for filling more than 1,150 different ministry spots within our Christian education program. We quit counting after we got to 1,150, so I know it is in excess of that. That doesn't mean that there are 1,150 people in these jobs; however, it does mean that there are that many different jobs to fill in order to cover all of our bases.

We do not have one recruiting strategy. Some churches try to use only certain ages for certain classes. We are not that sophisticated. We try to recruit any way we can. Sometimes one way seems to be more effective than another. Recruitment is always on my mind. I can never sit back and say, "There, I am finished for this year." I try to recruit for at least a year's period of time, but I want people to be thinking long-term rather than how quickly they can get this over with.

Workers for the Harvest

+ + + + + + +

It seems that every church is faced with the challenge of finding enough workers for the harvest. At Ward Church, we teach that *recruiting is everybody's business.* Every teacher needs to be on the lookout for others who could teach. However, the teaching assignment is not everybody's business. While we want people to be on the lookout for potential teachers and to make recommendations to us, our age group directors make the actual assignments and work with people in the final recruitment process. We have a tiny tots director, an early childhood ministries director, and a director of children's-level ministries, first through sixth grade. In each division, the director clears the names of prospective workers.

If the youth staff and the early childhood directors get the name of the same person, they are all free to present their ministry opportunity. We ask the prospective worker to choose the ministry where he feels that God is leading him. *The foundation of prayer must underlie everything that we do in recruitment.* We encourage people to pray for our staff and the new workers. We are helping people discover ministries from God, which is a sacred trust. So people are not just responsible to the Christian education staff; they are responsible to God for their performance. Therefore, we pray for the teachers and that they will serve to the best of their ability.

Heightening Awareness of the Importance of Teaching

+ + + + + + +

Our Christian education department uses many means to heighten awareness of the importance of teaching. We go into our *membership information classes* and present the teaching opportunities. We give an overview of these various opportunities for ministry. We have a *ministries booklet* that gives ministry descriptions and lists the requirements for each of those ministries. Also, in the membership information classes, we give a spiritual gifts test. We have what we call *spiritual gifts counselors* who meet with the people and answer their questions. We help people identify the areas where they are best equipped to serve.

We also believe that recruiting is helped a lot from the pulpit. Not that the pastor actually recruits from the pulpit, but it is his attitude toward our ministry that helps the recruitment process. For example, from time to time he might pray in the pastoral prayer for the folks who are serving and teaching, or he might encourage people to use their spiritual gifts as part of the sermon application. That certainly helps.

We try not to recruit people for specific tasks through a general want ad approach. We have found that the people who usually respond to these ads are not the ones that we feel ought to be there. Nevertheless, we periodically provide a listing of opportunities to keep the awareness level high so that church members know there is a place to serve as God calls them. One way we do this is with *bulletin inserts* that tell people how many workers are serving in different areas and what our needs may be. We do *video documentaries* in our classes and then periodically run those videos in the church's hallways. As people pass by, they can stop and see what is happening. Visibility is so important, and any avenue that heightens awareness is worth trying.

Sometimes we find long-term workers among people who have previously served in shorter assignments. After experiencing the joy of serving, some are more open to a long-term assignment. Vacation Bible School, for example, is one program where some people volunteer because it is not an ongoing commitment. Working on children's rallies or going on retreats are other good examples. We keep our eyes on these newly involved folks. If we see that they are good with children, we challenge them with additional opportunities.

Developing Potential Volunteers

+ + + + + + +

We are always looking for people who seem to work well with children. If we get a person's name and she has indicated some interest, then the coordinator for that area will contact her and try to discern whether or not she really does have an interest.

When we contact a prospective worker, *we invite her to come and see our ministries*. She can observe a class or look at our curriculum. We explain our passion for children, our philosophy of ministry, and the details of service. Then, if she is still interested, we have both videos and cassettes that she can use to become more acquainted with what we are doing. She can also view sample class sessions or actual training tapes. She learns how we teach children, age-group characteristics—a whole series of things.

If she still shows interest, an experienced master teacher will take that potential teacher under her wing. The prospective worker will observe a class session, even sitting alongside the teacher during the instruction process.

We also invite prospective workers and parents to *teacher training classes*. A parent may attend because he wants to know how to communicate better with his children. We feel that people can become better parents if they come to a training class. These events are primarily for skill development, but at the conclusion of a session, if someone feels that God is leading him to serve, we want to help that person take the next step.

Sometimes a person is approved, committed, and ready to teach, but we do not have a spot available. That doesn't happen as often as we would like, but it does happen. Other times we rush the process a little more because the need is greater. If we do not have a spot for someone, we usually find a spot such as an assistant in a department. Some who have had more experience are ready to go right away. Others need a little more time.

We often use teenagers in our children's ministry. Students who want to work in our ministry are required to participate in training. We offer a child-care clinic for those interested in working with infants and toddlers. If they prefer to work with early childhood, they must complete a junior teacher training class. When students are certified, showing that they are qualified to care for children, they are appointed as apprentices and used as junior teachers.

We do not use teenagers unless they are also involved in the teen program. Some youth like to hide out from their peers because they don't feel comfortable with their group, but we feel that it is important for them to be involved with people their own age. We do not use teenagers unless we feel they are mature enough to work with the children. Of course, this is a value judgment that our coordinator must make. When we step back and look at our ministry over time, we find that some of our best young adults teaching today began their ministries when they were still in their teens.

Serving Commandments

+ + + + + + +

We ask all of our workers to *sign a covenant* every year. They do not have to be church members, but they do have to be regular participants in the church family for at least six months. This general covenant talks about the quality of their life, their Christian character, and the fact that they are born again. They promise that they will not teach contrary to the stated doctrines of the church and will use the curriculum provided for them.

At Ward Church, *we seek a one-year commitment to service.* We recognize that people's lives and schedules can change; events happen that require people to leave before their commitment has been completed. Nevertheless, we want them to be thinking in terms of the school year plus the summer.

We recruit so that our new faculty is in place when the school year begins in the fall, so we do our heaviest recruitment during the summer. If we know in the spring or summer that a teacher will be leaving, we really like to have somebody come in and work with that teacher for at least a few weeks and to be in place before the new class arrives.

We recognize that people need to take vacations. They need to have times when they're not available to teach, and we make allowances for that. We use *substitute teachers* who help out when the regular teachers need a break. However, we do ask teachers to take their responsibility seriously and be faithful to their annual commitment.

Since many of our teachers work with minors, we ask them to complete a *background character form* and give us permission to secure a *criminal background check*. We want to know whether or not they have ever been perpetrators of any types of child abuse whether emotional, physical, or sexual. The background check, which is done through the Michigan State Police records, is required of anyone in the church who may work with a minor. If there are no problems, they are placed on a list that allows us to use them.

Assuring a Positive Experience for Teachers

+ + + + + + +

When we recruit teachers, we not only want a commitment from them, but we make a commitment that we will be there to assist them. *We promise to help them do the best job they can possibly do*. We firmly believe that effective teaching starts with relationships, so we encourage teachers to build positive relationships with their learners. That means we, as leaders, have to build effective relationships with our teachers if we expect them to build effective relationships with their learners.

It is our responsibility to *provide all of the curriculum and resources* that they need. We also *provide training for both new and continuing teachers*. We assist them in learning how to use the curriculum effectively, and try to help them understand the age-group characteristics of the children they are teaching. We do *preservice training* to give them help with teaching techniques and *in-service training* throughout the year. These are done by age-group levels, allowing us to deal with the needs of that particular age level. Teachers can also participate in a voluntary certification program called "Royalty." Special recognition is given to teachers who complete their five-point enrichment program.

Twice a year we put on a *resource fair* for early childhood and elementary teachers. Learning activity suggestions from our curriculum are worked on in advance. All of the supplies and materials are there along with the people who have prepared them. This helps new teachers and workers know what the material is going to look like and how it should be used.

The development of new teachers is also enhanced when we pair them with experienced teachers. In our children and youth ministries, we run our programs on a team basis. *Teachers function together as a team*, so that they are not lone rangers. We have found that when teachers pray together and become concerned for each other, they are more likely to continue in ministry for a longer time.

Periodically we *prepare lessons together*. Teachers bring their assignments and they work together in departmental teams. As they work in their groups, they learn how to tell the Bible lesson, how to do the memory work, and decide who is going to lead the singing and prayer time.

I once heard a Christian education veteran say that leaders shouldn't be making first-year mistakes over and over again. Instead, we need to be learning so that we are making second-year mistakes, then third-year mistakes, then fourth-year mistakes. We become more expert as we develop our gifts and skills.

Affirming Our Teachers

✝ ✝ ✝ ✝ ✝ ✝ ✝

We try to affirm teachers in a number of different ways. We give simple gifts and notes of appreciation. We have had seasonal parties, such as a holiday banquet at Christmas and an old-fashioned summer picnic. We hold appreciation dinners and programs. If they are sick, we visit them; if there is a death in their family, we send flowers. We find every way possible to affirm their work.

Occasionally we give them reminder-type gifts. Our logo, an apple with a heart in the center, is printed on all our gifts; for example, we had coffee mugs made with our logo and Henrietta Mears' statement, "First I learn to love my teacher, then I learn to love my teacher's God." All of our teachers are given one of these mugs.

We also provide them with canvas bags to put their Sunday school curriculum in. They carry the bags back and forth to church. At first I didn't think the bags were a very good idea, but the women on our staff thought it was a wonderful idea. I didn't think the men would carry them. Despite my misgivings, we went ahead with the idea and had the apple logo and the words "Ward Church Christian Ed Department" printed on the bags. I was surprised that the men carry those bags just like the women do! The bags have helped people recognize who the teachers in our church are.

A couple more gift examples include some chocolate hearts on a lollipop stick that we gave to our teachers around Valentine's Day. Each lollipop was accompanied with a little thank-you note. Another time we bought big, red apples. We went into the classes and departments, expressed words of appreciation for the teacher, and presented each teacher with a nice big, red apple. It was our way of saying, "Thank you for being available to teach."

We believe that teachers who feel appreciated and affirmed will in turn affirm the children they teach. And we want our members and children to see how important our teachers are to the life of our church. "Seeing is believing," and at Ward, we continually keep in the spotlight the good things that are happening through our volunteers.

✝ ✝ ✝ ✝ ✝ ✝ ✝

Ward Evangelical Presbyterian Church does an excellent job of keeping both the needs of children and the joys of teaching before the congregation. Frequently they highlight what is happening in the lives of children through their ministries. Likewise, they elevate the role of teaching, encouraging their teachers through many expressions of appreciation.

The leadership team at Ward Church demonstrates the principle that the more visible a ministry is, the more likely it is that people will consider the possibility of a call to that area of service. The more highly valued a program is, the more it will appeal to people. And the better known a recruiter is, the more likely a prospect will think about the ministry opportunity.

Ministry Resources

The following materials are used at Ward Evangelical Presbyterian Church in their Christian education ministries. Permission to use and adapt these resources in your congregation is granted. Duplication or distribution of these copyrighted materials for resale is prohibited.

CHILDREN'S WALK-THROUGH PROCEDURES

Sunday, March 10

At **each** hour, begin to line your children up at the classroom door approximately five minutes into the hour. You must leave your classroom no later than ten minutes into the hour. You must be in the narthex and ready to march down the center aisle 12 to 15 minutes into the hour.

At 8:00, leave your room by 8:10.
At 9:15, leave your room by 9:25.
At 10:45, leave your room by 10:55.
At 12:05, leave your room by 12:15.

We know not all children are in their classrooms on time. Early childhood teachers must leave one teacher in the classroom to stay with those who arrive late. Elementary classes should have at least one teacher remain in each department.

Early childhood classrooms will be provided with knotted ropes that morning for your children to hang on to as they walk. For the children's safety, and so that no one gets lost, USE THEM!

All classes must be certain to have one teacher at the front of the line and at least one at the rear as the children are walking to make sure we have no "stragglers."

PROCEDURE

Stand quietly with your children in the narthex. Monitors will be in the narthex to tell you where to stand. We will be forming TWO lines to go down the aisle.

Immediately after the offertory (choir bells will be ringing the song), we will begin our march. As soon as "This Little Light of Mine" begins to play, we will begin! Sing along and encourage the children to sing too!

The line on the right (facing the altar) will go up the center aisle at the same time as the line on the right. They will turn left at the altar, come back down the left center aisle, and return to their classrooms.

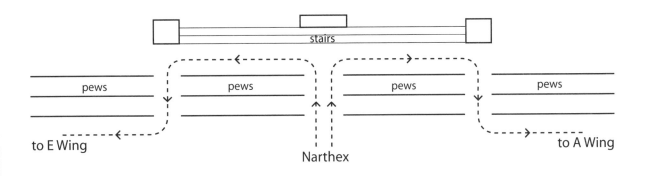

CHRISTIAN EDUCATION GOALS

In order for the student of Ward Evangelical Presbyterian Church Sunday school to achieve the best possible biblical and Christian education, the following goals are established as guidelines for cumulative progressive learning. To achieve these goals, the age groups will be developing Bible skills, Bible knowledge, and life response as described below:

Ages 2 - 3 Years

Bible Skills

Bible Knowledge and Life Response

* *

The Child Will:

1. Learn two finger plays.
2. Learn one song per quarter.
3. Learn one verse of Scripture per quarter.
4. Recognize the word "Bible."

1. Begin to associate God and the Lord Jesus with loving people and enjoyable activities.
2. Develop an awareness of the name of Jesus.
3. Associate Jesus with being loved, and feeling secure and loved at church by caring adults.

Ages 4 - 5 Years

Bible Skills

Bible Knowledge and Life Response

* *

The Child Will:

1. Recognize the word "Bible."
2. Know who wrote the Bible (God told men what to write).
3. Explain why God gave us His Word (His loving plan to forgive our sins and give us everlasting life).
4. Recognize at least one difference between the Old and New Testaments (e.g., Old Testament tells what happened before Jesus came; the New Testament tells what happened when Jesus was on earth and what happened after He went to Heaven).
5. Know at least ten Bible verses of the 12 studied this year.
6. Know ten finger plays and songs.

1. Know that God loves and cares for him and that God wants his trust and obedience.
2. Understand that God sent the baby Jesus, who grew to be the man Jesus.
3. Recognize that the church is a special place for him to learn about the greatness of God and the Lord Jesus.
4. Respond by demonstrating love to God and Jesus through kindness, helpfulness, and thankfulness to others.
5. Exhibit ways of being a helper at home and church.
6. Begin talking to God and Jesus through prayer.
7. Understand tithing and begin giving.

(continued)

Grades: 1st & 2nd (Primary)

Bible Skills

Bible Knowledge and Life Response

* *

The Child Will:

1. Name the first five books of the Old Testament.
2. Name the first four books of the New Testament.
3. Know the main themes of the Bible.
4. Memorize these selected Bible verses: 1 Corinthians 13:4, 5; Luke 2:3-14; Psalm 23 and 100.
5. Learn the Easter story.
6. Memorize at least four verses per quarter.
7. Recall familiar verses from previous chapters.
8. Know five songs.
9. Locate Bible references by using the contents page in the Bible.
10. Use a children's Bible dictionary.

1. Experience that God loves and cares for him.
2. Know that he can have Christ in his life.
3. Begin to learn to trust God.
4. Respond to God by thanking Him and serving others.
5. Be given a helping task in Sunday school class.
6. Learn to praise God using Scripture and personal devotions.
7. Begin to believe God's promises.
8. Begin to obey commands, and understand why God wants us to obey Him.
9. Be a prayer partner for one of the missionary children.
10. Know about four missionaries—where they serve and what they do.

Grades: 3rd & 4th (Middlers)

Bible Skills

Bible Knowledge and Life Response

* *

The Child Will:

1. Be able to name the first 17 books of the Old Testament and their divisions (e.g., Books of Law).
2. Be able to name the first 12 books of the New Testament and their divisions.
3. Memorize the Ten Commandments.
4. Learn one new verse per week.
5. Identify the basic theme/content of Genesis, the Psalms, the Gospels, and Acts.

1. Know that God loves and helps him.
2. Understand that God has a plan for his life.
3. Acknowledge that God sent His Son to be his Savior and Lord.
4. Begin to affirm to others a personal knowledge of Jesus Christ.
5. Choose to show God's love by obeying His Word (understand Scripture as a source of wisdom).

(continued)

6. Identify Old and New Testament personalities and events.
7. Understand the principle of tithing.
8. Understand the principles of worship and the purpose of the sacraments.

6. Know something about eight missionaries and the field in which they serve.
7. Tithe 10 percent of his allowance to the Lord.
8. Recognize that God has a special purpose for him.
9. Know at least two Ward missionaries.
10. Understand what it means to be a witness.

Grades: 5th & 6th (Juniors)

Bible Skills

Bible Knowledge and Life Response

* *

The Child Will:

1. Be able to list all of the books of the Bible in order.
2. Identify the major divisions of the Bible.
3. Name the books in each division.
4. Use a Bible concordance and Bible atlas.
5. Identify the basic themes/content of Exodus, Joshua, 1 & 2 Samuel, Proverbs, Romans, Galatians, James, and 1 John.
6. Memorize one verse each week, plus Psalms 19, 24, 33, and 150.
7. Understand stories of the Bible personalities and be able to parallel them to people today.

1. Acknowledge that God wants His people to trust, love, and obey Him.
2. Know that God helps each person to mature through His Word, church, and family.
3. Begin to serve in the church.
4. Know how to become a missionary.
5. Understand what a disciple is.
6. Be able to share a personal faith and to lead a friend to Christ.
7. Understand scriptural principles for decision making.
8. Know what is good for our bodies; why we shouldn't take drugs, drink, smoke, or be involved in premarital sex.
9. Develop close peer friendships within the church.

TEACHERS AND PARENTS: A PARTNERSHIP

Often as administrators, we hear: "If only the parents would . . ." and "If only the teachers would. . . ." These are unfortunate comments that develop when the roles of teacher and parent are misunderstood.

Our job as Sunday school teachers is to support the parents in their job of spiritually educating their children. Some families teach spiritual truths; however, others are ill-equipped to do so.

Obviously, we see only a portion of the children's lives. It is crucial that we stand in partnership with the parent, not in criticism or competition. A great deal can be done to help parents in their task.

Communicate

If the child's parent(s) drops him off and picks him up, be sure to introduce yourself. Let the parents know you are glad their child is in your class. Show interest in family concerns, but don't believe everything the child tells you about his family life! You'd be surprised what the parents hear about your Sunday school class!

Let the parents know what their child is studying, and how the parents can reinforce the lessons. The curriculum provides a "letter to parents" on which you can easily drop a quick note. Look for opportunities to share ideas with parents who are open to receiving them.

Phone calls or notes to absentees let *parents* know the importance of bringing their child on a regular basis, and can also give you insights on their home situations. Home visits are a powerful "I care about you" statement from teachers. A team of children's teachers visit weekly; see Cindy if you would like to join them.

If a child in your class has special needs, the situation can accelerate to the point where you need help from the parent. Rather than calling and saying, in essence, "Your child is a brat!" approach the parent with concern that you seem unable to adequately meet his needs and "would [the parent] have any suggestions for you?" This also tells the child that his parents and his teacher are "in cahoots," and in itself can provide more accountability for good behavior. It may be the child is being "helped" at home with the same areas of needed growth, and you can reinforce what the parent or school is already attempting.

GUIDELINES FOR DISCIPLINE

Children who need redirecting are often seen as an interruption and bother in our teaching time. It is important to instead remember them as an *opportunity*, knowing that God desires to use this moment to continue to mold them . . . and to teach us!

Many of our classroom problems can be avoided by careful planning. An unprepared teacher is more on edge, less exciting, and communicates that this class isn't very important. No wonder, then, that the children agree! Know what you want to do, for how long, and have all your materials ready to go. Unprepared teachers open the door to misbehavior.

Be on time! Whoever is in the class first, "wins"! If the children beat you to class, they will have already determined their behavior and standards for the hour. You need to be ready with activities to channel their energy the minute they walk in the door.

Teachers who push the attention span of children are also asking for restless behavior. If one or two are restless, deal with them. If more than two are restless, take a look at the class time you have planned. Perhaps you need to build in more activity, less talk and answer time, and more opportunities for the children to be actively involved.

There are many "under the table" ways to approach the restlessness that usually precedes disruption:

1. Be sure your classroom is arranged so that you can "reach" every child. Do not stand or sit where you have poor eye contact. Move about as the hour progresses, so you may be close to each child during the hour. Have the children move from chairs on the floor to chairs and tables for the various activities.

2. Remove any distractions. Have children place unnecessary supplies under their table or on a special supply table. Leave the area in front of them free from clutter to help focus their attention.

3. When a child is becoming restless, casually move toward him. Do not lunge or threaten. A soft hand on the shoulder or loving touch of the arm may be all the redirection he needs.

4. Drop a child's name in the middle of a sentence, or ask him a question, but be careful not to embarrass him or put him on the spot. Keep your tone light.

(continued)

5. Shift speeds—speed up or slow down what you are doing. The change in pace may be all it takes to bring the child's attention back.

6. Shift activity. Frankly, some things we do simply "bomb." If the general restlessness is growing, it is time to move to something else. Always have extra activities in your "back pocket" for such moments!

Sometimes, these approaches are not enough. If a child's restlessness is bothering more than just you, it may be time to move to a more direct approach. "First I learn to love my teacher, then I learn to love my teacher's God." In any disturbance, it is important to first pray that God will help you to show His love and care in the midst of confrontation.

Tell the child what you would like him to do, and give him a good reason. Simply redirect his *actions*. Many such children are eager to "help" if it is time to pass out materials or hold something for everyone to see. He needs a good reason for changing his activity, not just "we don't do that in church."

Talk to the child individually about what he did, and ask why you would not find that behavior acceptable. Ask what he should have done instead.

Develop a set of consequences, but ones that meet the misbehavior; e.g., the consequence for misuse of materials is losing the privilege of using them.

For a repeat offender, the Sunday school staff is available to assist you. We may be aware of that child's special needs. Do as much as you can to build a relationship with the child: calling him, visiting him at home, making a point to learn about him and make him feel loved.

What is "Royalty"? It is a five-point voluntary certification program for our Christian education workers.

"ROYALTY" can be attained through

1. **R**eading
2. **O**bserving another class
3. **Y**early conference and/or workshop attendance
4. **A**ssessment of your teaching, and
5. **L**eadership training: attending a minimum number of meetings and development opportunities

After you have completed the requirements, you will be awarded a "golden apple pin," be honored at a teacher's meeting, and have your name and picture appear in the *Cornerstone*. The main purpose of "Royalty" is to challenge yourself to be a more qualified teacher and to encourage others to take that same exemplary challenge.

More detailed information about this program is available in the Christian Education office in the "Royalty" flyer.

Chapter Six

Get on Board: A Master Teaching Approach

Mt. Paran Church of God
Atlanta, Georgia

"Why do we have to visit another church?" your son asked about three hours ago. No doubt he was still reacting to the boring class held in the dingy basement of the church you visited last week. But now, running toward you, is an excited child. "Mom, you can't believe how great this church is. Can we stay here? Let's not look at any other churches!"

Your child just came out of Grand Central Station, a premier children's ministry at Mt. Paran Church of God, Atlanta, Georgia. This high-energy program for elementary students incorporates all of a child's senses using puppets and unique characters to teach life principles from God's Word. This is not Mt. Paran's only program for children, but it does illustrate Mt. Paran's principle that quality programming with a solid "identity" does not require preset teacher-student ratios. Rather, the number of volunteers needed to run any particular ministry really depends on the nature of each specific program.

Pastor Norman Cruikshank, former children's minister and the one who implemented Grand Central Station at Mt. Paran, tells us about the ministry and its challenges at this exciting church.

Megachurch Challenge

+ + + + + + +

Mt. Paran Church of God has nearly four thousand members. As many large churches have discovered, megachurches make a good place to hide. Some families attend only to take advantage of the services offered, with the adults acting as spectators. In proportion to smaller churches, we have a smaller percentage of volunteers. Thus a challenge at Mt. Paran is to minister to a large number of kids with a smaller yet able group of volunteers.

In our church, most kids come at 11:00 A.M, which is a huge service for us. So we have chosen to utilize a select team of volunteers to minister to a large number of children. This may not be the best way to personally disciple children and teach the Word, but we do have children who come each week excited about their program. They come back excited because of the quality and energy of Grand Central Station. A program ministering to four hundred children typically struggles to find the fifty plus volunteers needed to lead and teach that number of kids. But with a *large event format*, an engaging worship and learning experience can be provided by a team of only a dozen leaders.

The starting place in promoting our children's ministry is to keep before our people how important our children are to us. We place high value on our children's ministry. One way we emphasize this is with a *children's ministry logo*. Just as companies spend thousands of dollars on a logo that will identify their product, we, too, want our children's ministries to stick out in people's minds. Our logo is a train, which signifies our whole premise of "training children in the way they should go."

People constantly need to be reminded of our vision. The purpose for children's ministry is spelled out clearly in our handbook, which communicates our rationale for working with children. We paint a picture for them of what children's ministry means to us.

We believe in ministering to the whole life of the child. We have tried to define our ministry goals and objectives very clearly. These goals and objectives are all written out plainly to fulfill Proverbs 22:6. Many people make the mistake of taking somebody else's program, then trying to implement that program in their church. We make sure that we know what we want to accomplish before we start trying to get volunteers. The bottom line for any of us in leadership is to target the areas of ministry that we believe are important, then start searching out specific types of people to work in those ministries.

Praying Them In, Praying Them Out

+ + + + + + +

Prayer has always been an ongoing part of our ministry. "God, send us laborers," I pray. "We need this kind of person. And if the person who's there is not the right person, please send us the right person."

The Lord is faithful in raising up people for His ministry. God seems to order our steps and put people in our path, so we have determined to wait until the right people come along. This doesn't mean that we don't do our part in cultivating people, but we'd rather make other adjustments than put somebody in a classroom when we do not have peace about that person. As we've practiced this approach, God has faithfully brought good people to us.

When we first meet with prospective workers, we present them with an overview of the activities and opportunities in children's ministries. We tell them, "We'll let you call us about your possible commitment," and then we leave them alone. We have found that when they call us, their commitment level is predictably higher. If we have to keep calling them back and asking, "Well, are you interested or not?" then we're probably going to be calling them every Sunday. We don't twist arms anymore.

Volunteers are much more effective when they come to us. Most of our really good teachers are people who found us; we didn't find them. God sends the right people.

Relational Recruitment

+ + + + + + +

Experience has proven that blanket calls for volunteers are our least effective means of getting quality volunteers. The most effective means is finding workers one at a time. It has taken us several years to build a good team, but when we have the right people in the right places, they usually stay with us for the long haul.

We encourage our teachers to find members within the church, people they know whom they can draw into service. When this happens, our professional staff can spend more time interviewing and training because our volunteers are making a lot of the initial contacts for our children's ministry.

We also have *new member luncheons* that follow new member orientation. A lot of potential teachers are met through table conversations at those meetings. As we begin to talk with people about what the Lord is doing through children's ministry, their eyes light up and they give us their attention. As a matter of fact, our preschool director came out of a conversation during a lunch like that. The relational aspect is so important. When we connect with people, they are usually like-minded with us.

Using Summer Programs to Find Volunteers

✠ ✠ ✠ ✠ ✠ ✠ ✠

At Mt. Paran, *we ask teachers to make a one-year commitment.* However, we have found that teachers in traditional Sunday school classes do a lot better when they serve only during the school year—September to May. We let them off for June, July, and August while we run our summer schedule.

There are several things we do differently during the summer. Since our kids come and go all summer long, our summer program doesn't require that they be here every week. Programs such as the Pioneer Clubs, which build on the teaching and learning done the previous week, aren't held during the summer. However, we have Bible Bowl—a type of a Scripture memory drill utilizing a team-teaching environment—that works great during the summer. We also offer a fifth-grade discipleship class. A staff pastor teaches doctrine, foundations of salvation, and Scripture, which helps us get to know where these kids are coming from.

Another thing we do differently is that we combine the first and second grade classes, and the third and fourth grade classes. These classes can end up being rather large, but attendance patterns during the summer are often sporadic anyway, so the class sizes are usually manageable. We make sure we place teachers in the classrooms who can handle a large group of children. Since schoolteachers are much more available in the summer than they are during the school year, we use a lot of these experienced people in our summer classes. This again illustrates our philosophy that certain types of programs, staffed by master teachers, can minister to a larger group of students than the normally expected one to eight teacher-student ratios most Sunday schools struggle to achieve.

Our summer programs—VBS and camp programs—are very strong. A lot of people will volunteer for one-time events such as VBS or camp because they are big, high-visibility projects and the time commitment is short. We use these opportunities as *feeder programs* for our other volunteer needs; for example, during the spring we put cards in the pews indicating our need for volunteers to serve just for the summer. We list the different summer activities such as VBS, camp, and various outings and trips. The card may say "chaperone sign-up." When people indicate an interest in volunteering, they are interviewed and their names are kept on file.

We make working with VBS easy to do. It's volunteer friendly. There are six to eight teams and the teachers are basically team leaders. The volunteers lead the kids from activity to activity, but an experienced teacher gives the lesson. As long as each team has a team leader we know, we're comfortable placing a nonmember or less experienced volunteer with that leader. This skirts around our policy a little but during large events, we sometimes don't have many options. We are willing to use an available parent or individual who is asking, "Can I help?"

The summer programs give us opportunities to begin building relationships with new people who have not taught before. When fall comes and new Sunday school teachers are needed, we usually find several good people from these programs. For example, one summer we found a wonderful teacher who had done a great job during VBS. Later in the summer, we called to see if she would consider teaching the fifth graders, and she accepted the position. She is great and seems to be in it for long haul!

Camp does the same thing for us. We take twenty to thirty workers to camp and develop relationships with them. A lot of these people find their way into our children's ministry because our time together became an opening for service. They got a chance to see who we are, catch our vision, and experience what working with kids is all about.

Interviewing Prospective Workers

+ + + + + + +

When people become members of the church, we give them a *Partners in Ministry Inventory Form*. They fill out the areas of ministry they are interested in. People will often check something off without really knowing what they want to do, so part of our job is to clarify an area where they can minister effectively. Each person will be contacted individually to talk about service opportunities. Say, for example, we have someone who isn't sure where she wants to serve. Perhaps she checked off ten different areas (she was supposed to check only three). We will contact her and say, "I am following up to find out if you are still interested in serving and to help you select an area of service." *We then conduct an interview to help her find the best ministry fit.* All prospective preschool and grade-school workers are interviewed by the children's minister. While this process is rather cumbersome, we feel it is our responsibility to know who is working with our children.

Most of the time we can find out what kind of individual they are just by the interview. We become acquainted with them and learn about their relationship to God. Occasionally we have found that a prospect is not even a Christian and have had the opportunity to lead that person to the Lord during the interviewing process. Obviously these people are not placed in classrooms as lead teachers, but they may work as assistants, so we still walk them through the qualifications listed in the handbook.

Three things are essential for either paid or volunteer staff:

1. *They must be born-again believers.*

2. *They must be church members.* Our policy states that people have to be members of Mt. Paran for at least six months before they are allowed to work in a classroom as a teacher. Because of the pressing need, we have sometimes skirted the six-month rule. Nevertheless, they do have to be a member. And before they are introduced as a teacher of any type, they have to go through the application process.

3. *They must have a personal interview with the director of children's ministry.* This applies to all people working with children from birth through fifth grade. And they must complete the ministry application form.

Sometimes an interview will result in an immediate placement because the volunteer will say, "I know what I want to do. I want to teach first grade." Or, "I want to teach on Sunday morning at 9:45." But nine times out of ten, we're simply introducing prospective volunteers to the program at our first meeting. They learn what we do and the types of programs we offer. We walk them through those programs so they know exactly what our children's ministry offers them.

Our handbook has a job description for each position. It lays out the particulars of the teaching task. Before a teacher even steps into the classroom, he ought to know the cost of his commitment. That saves us a lot of headaches down the line. We don't have as many phone calls at 8:00 A.M. Sunday saying, "I'm not coming in."

On the *ministry application form*, we provide a temperament chart for each person to complete. Obviously it is not a comprehensive analysis, but we do want to know about their gifts and basic temperament. We ask them to answer questions about children's ministry. We ask for their testimony. Since we are in a position that requires us to filter through a lot of people, we can tell a lot through such a procedure. Time restricts us from being able to do an exhaustive background check, but at the same time, our concern for our children constrains us to ask significant questions. In addition, we call at least three references to find out if a prospective volunteer is who she says she is. We also ask if the references would recommend her for a volunteer position in a classroom.

Protecting Our Children

+ + + + + +

One of the most important things we face is the need for child protection. This is an especially hot issue for parents who bring their small children. Over the last two years, child protection has taken precedence over anything else that we've done. Without a doubt, it has caused us to revamp the way we recruit volunteers. There was a day when we could open the door and say, "All right, whoever wants to teach. . . ." But if we did that today, we could end up in court with a lawsuit on our hands.

This is more than a litigious issue; *genuine concern for the well-being of every child is a priority.* In the nursery, we want to see volunteers wearing gloves when changing diapers. We want to see our workers disinfecting the changing table and nursery toys. This is all for child protection—to prevent diseases from being transmitted among children. Our paid staff members are required to go through first aid and CPR training with the American Red Cross. All of these procedures are discussed in our handbook.

At an initial screening meeting, volunteers are presented with classroom procedures and rules. For example, they are informed that we have a minimum of two people in each classroom. We explain why we have windows in all of our doors. We have tried to create an environment that would thwart a child molester looking for a place to operate.

We also inform our teachers what Georgia law requires about reporting a child who has a laceration, cigarette burn, or bruise that is suspicious. Georgia state law doesn't presently require a criminal background check, so we don't add that extra burden to our volunteers. But we do take the time to discuss this important matter with our people because they need to know how we value and protect our children. We need assurance that they are in agreement with our concerted child protection efforts before they ever step into the classroom.

Implementing these protection policies has made the door narrower for volunteers to enter. We have created a lot of filters. But the volunteers we have are all on the same page regarding child protection.

Determining Teacher-Student Ratios

+ + + + + + +

Families come to a church if it has a good ministry for their children. Parents will sacrifice their own needs for the needs of their kids. An adequate teaching staff is important to parents, but the *number of teachers needed for any program depends on what we are trying to accomplish.* We use close ratios in our nursery and in our preschool. As a matter of fact, our nursery will close down rooms when we have exceeded the maximum number of children per caregiver.

In a traditional type of program, we normally work with a one-to-eight ratio with elementary-age children. But when we can put more kids together and operate with two or three adults, that's what we do. As I mentioned before, *our premier children's program does not have "traditional" teaching attached to it.* Grand Central Station utilizes drama and puppets, and has more of a theater-type feel to it. When we first showcased the program, we brought in a team to model its value. People can get excited about a program when they understand the purpose behind what they are doing. When leaders know what needs to be accomplished and how to get there, many people will get on board. So we invited two to three hundred people from our children's ministry to observe this innovative program. As we polled the response of the people to Grand Central Station, many said, "I can do this." That night we found most of our volunteers for Grand Central Station, people who are gifted differently than the teachers who work in a classroom with a standard curriculum.

Sunday morning is not going to meet the needs of every child. Summer is not going to meet the needs of every child. But when we consider the whole pie, we can see that we are able to meet particular needs throughout the year via individual programs. Sunday mornings and Wednesday nights are pieces of that pie; so are the children's camp, the special events, and the concerts. All of these things create programs that meet the needs of the whole life of the child. We need volunteers for each and every part.

Training Our Volunteers

+ + + + + + +

Training is one of the most frustrating areas for any pastor because you are faced with thirty to forty minutes to teach something that probably needs half a day to teach. A few years ago, several of us were faced with that frustration, so we birthed the Atlanta Sunday School Convention. Once a year, we pay for all of our teachers to attend the convention. For two days, they can pick and choose courses and receive the training they need.

Our most successful time of meeting with leaders has been after church on Sundays. We have tried Tuesday night and Thursday night, but in Atlanta, most people don't go outside the house after 6 P.M. So we don't even try to do anything during evenings anymore. However, we have found that 90 percent of our people are here on Sunday morning, so we have a potluck after church every other month or once a quarter. We use these mealtimes for training, but I've also found them to be valuable for pure fellowship with our people.

During one of these lunches, some of our people shared their testimonies. It was powerful and very moving for our children's workers to hear what some of their peers have gone through. On another Sunday, we simply went around the room and prayed a blessing over each of the teachers. They were just like sponges; they soaked that up.

When it comes to policies and procedures specific to our church, we disseminate that information during those Sunday luncheons. However, we typically use the time for building skills. We use a mentoring type of training; first they watch us perform a skill, and then they do it. It's a modeling approach to training versus a content approach. We'd rather aim at the passion—the heart, the team building—than just show them an outline of three things on an overhead, which are often forgotten anyway.

Valuing Our Children

+ + + + + + +

All around us we see the destruction that the enemy has wrought in kids' lives. What kind of message is this sending to the church? The message we hear is, "Get them while they are young." This compels us even more to try to inculcate God's Word into these young lives.

At Mt. Paran, *we elevate ministry to children.* Many churches pour extraordinary

107

resources into their adult members. The best rooms are reserved for the "paying customers." You see, children never complain about the out-of-date furnishings or the lack of quality instruction they are given. In essence, they are the most cooperative members of a congregation. But they are the most valuable! We should be aggressively pursuing the children of our churches because as go the children, so goes the church!

In 1650, an educator named John Comenius said, "Soft wax can be molded and remolded; hard wax will crumble. The young tree can be planted, replanted, trimmed and bent to any shape; not so the grown. So also the hands and limbs of man can be trained for art and craft only during his childhood, as long as sinews are soft. . . . In the same way piety must be implanted into the hearts during infancy lest it not root. If we want to educate a person in virtue, we must polish him at a tender age." The Bible tells us the same thing in Proverbs 22:6: "Train a child in the way he should go, and when he is old he will not turn from it" (*New International Version*).

Our children are our most valuable resource; we should treat them that way. At Mt. Paran, we are compelled to actively draw children into a vital relationship with Jesus Christ. For this reason, when we recruit people to teach we are inviting them to pursue a high calling. The result of their work, in the lives of children, will last forever.

+ + + + + +

Through Grand Central Station, Mt. Paran Church of God has learned that a children's theme, including a personalized logo, adds visibility and value to their program. The high-energy, captivating weekly event led by master teachers has also reduced the number of volunteers needed in their overall ministry.

Amassing bodies according to a chart on teacher/student ratios does not assure quality programming. But the right people in the right ministry will create a dynamic learning environment. Diversity within children's ministry will require some programs to use close teacher/student ratios, while other programs can operate with a large teacher/student ratio. The bottom line in staffing is that the nature of a program should always determine the number of volunteers needed.

Ministry Resources

The following materials are used at Mt. Paran Church of God in their Christian education ministries. Permission to use and adapt these resources in your congregation is granted. Duplication or distribution of these copyrighted materials for resale is prohibited.

Purpose

The purpose of the children's ministry is to provide a quality atmosphere of growth and development for children of all ages by:

1. Providing positive role models.
2. Offering exciting opportunities for instruction in God's Word.
3. Conducting monthly activities, seasonal outings, and special events.
4. Training adults to lead, disciple, teach, and counsel children.
5. Mobilizing children for world mission involvement.

Children's Ministry

The purpose of the children's ministry is to provide quality programs and activities that will instill biblical principles into the whole life of the child. For more information, contact the director of children's ministry.

Sunday School

Classes for children in preschool (K3–K5) through fifth grade are provided during the 9:00 and 11:00 A.M. services. These programs provide an intimate environment for children to learn basic principles from Scripture in a more traditional Sunday school environment. These classes are:

Grand Central Station (Grades one through five)

This exciting grade-school program incorporates all the child's senses using puppets and unique characters to teach life principles from God's Word. Meeting on Sunday mornings at 9:00 and 11:00 A.M., children from first to fifth grades learn how to reach out to their community.

Noah's Ark (K3 through K5)

This fast-paced preschool program takes children to a place where "Noah," a weathered seaman, lives with a host of animals and Oakly, a talking tree. Through various situations, the animals learn how God wants them to live. This program is held Sundays at 9:00 and 11:00 A.M.

Wednesday Evenings

The Wednesday night program for grade-school students operates on a quarterly schedule. Two quarters serve as "practice night" for the spring and Christmas musicals. The other quarters include special training and worship classes with the children's pastor.

Preschool is a fully structured classroom program for preschool students. It meets Wednesday evenings and includes singing, crafts, games, and Bible stories.

Nursery Program

Nursery programs are available during all Sunday services and Wednesday evening services. Nursery rooms are located on the first floor of the west wing next to the sanctuary.

(continued)

Special Programs

Puppet/Drama Team

This group of adults and teens uses its talents and gifts to perform for children's church and other special outreach programs throughout the year for Grand Central Station and Noah's Ark. A specialized group of puppeteers comprises "Puppet Express," our puppet outreach team that performs in schools, neighborhoods, and nursing homes.

Super Saturdays

During the school year, first through fifth graders take monthly trips to places like Scitrek, Zoo Atlanta, and Stone Mountain. These trips provide opportunities for both children and adults to build lasting relationships. Super Saturdays are really "super" times for moms and dads to get involved with what their children are doing.

Super Tuesdays

During the summer months, kids of all ages (including preschool) take bimonthly trips for fun, recreation, learning, and fellowship.

Vacation Bible School

Each year, Super Kids Week provides an opportunity for the children of the church to reach out to surrounding communities. A series of high-energy rallies are planned and the children compete in the Bible Bowl program. Preschool classes are also offered in the traditional Vacation Bible School format.

Hallowed Be Thy Name Festival

This event is an alternative to Halloween and invites the community to join the church in celebrating Christ using a festival format. There are rides, games, music, food, and fun for children of all ages.

Children's Musicals

Each spring and at Christmas, the first through fifth graders have the opportunity to use their gifts in a full-scale musical production performed for the entire church. The preschool choir also performs three to four times a year. Both age groups use Wednesday evenings as rehearsal times.

Summer Camp

Children in first through fifth grades are given an opportunity to participate in a week-long camping experience featuring various recreational activities (swimming, canoeing, archery, puppets, and camp crafts). Christian fellowship and personal development are the results of this event.

PHILOSOPHY, GOAL, AND OBJECTIVES OF CHILDREN'S MINISTRY

PHILOSOPHY

That if you train up a child in the way that he/she should go, when they are older, they will not turn from it (Proverbs 22:6).

GOAL

To provide quality programs and activities that will enable us to instill biblical principles and values into the whole life of a child.

OBJECTIVES

- To provide positive role models for children to follow.

- To provide opportunities for instruction in God's Word.

- To provide a safe and nurturing environment where children are accepted and loved.

- To train and provide a diversified team of volunteers and paid staff for leadership, teaching, and discipleship.

- To ensure the safety and well-being of all children while in our care.

- To provide facilities and programs that are age-appropriate and inviting.

- To provide opportunities for relationships to form between parents, leaders, and children through periodic trips, gatherings, and activities.

- To reach out into our surrounding communities with programs that introduce children and families to Jesus Christ.

- To involve children in the ministry of the whole church.

MINISTRY DESCRIPTION FOR CHILDREN'S WORKERS

Purpose

A children's ministry worker's main goal is to be a model. Jesus said, "Let your light so shine among men, that they may glorify your Father in Heaven" (Matthew 5:16). You are influencing the lives of children. This is a very high calling. In James 3:1, the Bible admonishes us, "Not many of you should presume to be teachers, my brothers, because you know that we who teach will be judged more strictly." If you work with children in any capacity, you are teaching them. Your purpose is to model Jesus Christ.

Qualifications of a Children's Ministry Worker (Paid and Volunteer)

A. Must be a born-again believer.
B. Must be a member of Mount Paran in good standing for at least six months.
C. Must have a personal interview with the director of children's ministries.
D. Must complete an Application for Ministry Involvement, have references checked, and possibly submit to a background check.

Ministry Responsibilities of a Children's Ministry Worker

A. Training
1. Attend any scheduled training meetings for your department. These happen about six times a year. There are also periodic training seminars and conferences available to those who seek to further their skills with children.
2. Nursery workers are required to take a CPR class through the Red Cross. Mt. Paran will pay for these classes for all paid nursery employees.
3. Must be familiar with all policies regarding communicable diseases, bodily fluids, and child protection policies.

B. Arrival Time
Arrive at least *twenty minutes prior* to the beginning of your class time. You should be ready to receive children at this time. Parents get anxious when there is no one to greet their child.

(continued)

C. Absences

Call ahead of time when you are going to be absent so a replacement can be secured. It is understandable that absences will occur among children's ministry workers. Please give us as much notice as possible. In the event of a sudden illness or emergency, please call the church and leave word with the operator or the appropriate department:

1. Nursery
2. Preschool
3. Grade school

D. Duration of Commitment

We ask that you give at least a one-year commitment to your area of service (volunteers only).

E. "Go the Second Mile"

1. Follow up on students. Try to send cards whenever possible.
2. Pray for your class every week before you come to teach.
3. Involve yourself in extracurricular activities that involve your class whenever possible.

F. Personal Life

1. Exhibit a lifestyle that would be pleasing to God throughout the week.
2. Must attend one service a week when not serving.

G. Discipline in the Classroom

1. Never strike a child under any circumstances.
2. If there are children who cannot be dealt with due to special handicaps, see the director of your department.
3. Remember: If you don't control your classroom, the children will.

H. "Two Adult Rule"

1. Two adults must be in a classroom during any church activity.
2. If a male is teaching, the other leader must be a female.

I. Suspicious Behavior (See Child Abuse & Molestation)

Behavior exhibited by a child or adult leader that is suspicious should be reported immediately to the director of your department.

J. Bathroom Usage

There should be an adult within earshot of the bathrooms to ensure that children do not linger in the bathrooms and make it back to class safely.

(continued)

K. Unapproved Workers in the Classroom

There should not be any children or adults in a classroom unless they have gone through proper procedures for working as an assistant or a classroom teacher.

L. Problems in the Classroom

1. Parents who have upset children will be allowed to stay for a short period of time until their child adjusts. However, parents are not allowed to stay through the entirety of the class. If their child will not adjust, they should be encouraged to take the child with them to the service or leave them in the classroom.
2. If a child is left and continues to cry persistently, the parents should be sought out so that the child does not disrupt the entire class. Please contact the director of your department so that the child's parents may be contacted.
3. Preschool children's parents can be contacted via the Number Paging System. This should be used in emergency situations ONLY! Only the director may input numbers into the keypad, which is located in the nursery office.

M. Ratio of Teachers to Children

If the ratio ever exceeds the following for any classroom, please notify the director of your department immediately:

Birth–12 months	1 to 3
12–24 months	1 to 4
Ages 3–5	1 to 6/8
Grade School	1 to 12/15

N. Dismissing Children From Classrooms

All children in fifth grade and below should be dismissed only with an approved adult or guardian (see "Checkout" Procedures).

The Mount Paran Preventive Goals for reducing child abuse and communicable diseases are threefold:

1. To provide protective care for our children and youth.
2. To maintain proper supervision and training for both compensated and volunteer youth and children's workers.
3. To provide every precaution to protect Mount Paran Church of God against any liability with regard to child abuse and communicable diseases.

Screening Procedures

I. Volunteer Workers

A. Church Membership

All volunteers who provide supervision and discipline of minors must be members of Mount Paran Church of God for at least six (6) months prior to volunteer services. The initial step of the membership process will be the requirement to attend the membership orientation class and successfully complete the Ministry Inventory questionnaire.

B. Application for Ministry Involvement

All volunteers who provide supervision and discipline of minors shall complete in entirety an Application for Ministry Involvement. In this application, persons will be asked to provide photo identification, personal references, and authorization for Mount Paran Church of God to request background name checks from law enforcement agencies.

C. Pastoral Interview

After favorable verification of all references and background checks, an interview is scheduled with the appropriate ministry supervisor. Upon a positive interview, the applicant's intent to engage in ministry will be made known to the Mount Paran administrative staff for consultation regarding any possible unknown present situations or questionable past behavior.

D. Formal Commissioning

Once the applicant has successfully completed and been approved in all screening procedures, he or she will be allowed to function in the capacity as a volunteer leader who supervises and disciplines minors. Indication is made by the leadership body and existing departmental ministry team by the appropriate ministry supervisors.

II. Compensated Workers

A. Application for Ministry Involvement

All compensated workers who provide supervision and discipline of minors shall complete in entirety an Application for Ministry Involvement. In this application, persons will be asked to provide photo identification, personal references, and authorization for Mount Paran Church of God to request background name checks from law enforcement agencies.

(continued)

B. Pastoral Interview

After favorable verification of all references and background checks, an interview is scheduled with the appropriate ministry supervisor. Upon a positive interview, the applicant's intent to engage in ministry will be made known to the Mount Paran administrative staff for consultation regarding any possible unknown present situations or questionable behavior.

C. Formal Commissioning

Once the applicant has successfully completed and been approved in all screening procedures, he or she will be allowed to function in the capacity as a compensated worker who supervises and disciplines minors. Indication is made by the leadership body and existing departmental ministry team by the appropriate ministry supervisors.

III. Parachurch Ministries

A. Application for Ministry Involvement

All parachurch ministry workers who provide supervision and discipline of minors shall complete in entirety an Application for Ministry Involvement. In this application, persons will be asked to provide photo identification, personal references, and authorization for Mount Paran Church of God to request background name checks from law enforcement agencies.

B. Pastoral Interview

After favorable verification of all references and background checks, an interview is scheduled with the appropriate ministry supervisor. Upon a positive interview, the applicant's intent to engage in ministry will be made known to the Mount Paran administrative staff for consultation regarding any possible unknown present situations or questionable behavior.

C. Formal Commissioning

Once the applicant has successfully completed and been approved in all screening procedures, he or she will be allowed to function in the capacity as a compensated worker who supervises and disciplines minors. Indication is made by the leadership body and existing departmental ministry team by the appropriate ministry supervisors.

Training

I. On-Site Training

All compensated and volunteer workers with minors will be required to attend all training sessions regarding child abuse and communicable diseases. Workers especially need to know the following:

   The definition of child abuse
   Sexual and physical abuse symptoms
   What constitutes inappropriate conduct
   Church policies that govern working with children and youth
   The civil and criminal consequences of misconduct
   Rationale behind screening procedures

(continued)

Periodic training sessions will be provided to update workers of any changes to Mount Paran Church policies or state regulations. All compensated and volunteer workers are expected to attend all specially called departmental meetings and the total leadership meeting with the senior pastor.

All compensated and volunteer nursery workers shall adhere to the policies prescribed in the *Mount Paran Ministry Procedures for Nursery and Children's Workers Manual.* All youth leaders shall adhere to the policies and guidelines prescribed in the *Youth Ministry Leadership Manual.*

II. Off-Site Training

Mount Paran Church of God requires that all compensated workers with minors be trained in CPR and health-related procedures that are necessary for their safety and care while working with minors. All volunteer workers with minors will be provided an opportunity for training advancement in CPR and health-related procedures. Mount Paran will also update all workers with current state policies and laws regarding working with minors, especially in the areas of child abuse protection and communicable diseases.

Supervision and Reporting Procedures

Churches can use reasonable care in selecting workers, but still be liable for injuries sustained during church activities on the basis of negligent supervision. Negligent supervision refers to a failure to exercise reasonable care in the supervision of church workers and church activities. The following are supervisory policies and reporting procedures for Mount Paran Church of God:

I. Supervision Procedures

A. The Two-Adult Rule
Two adult supervisors should be present during any church activity. Preferably one of these adults would be a parent of one of the participating youth or children, or at minimum, someone over eighteen years of age.

B. Obtaining Parental Permission
Church staff or volunteer workers should obtain consent of the child's parent or guardian before going out alone with that child or spending time with a child in an unsupervised situation. Parental permission is needed for all church-sponsored programs or activities involving minors that would require leaving the church property. This is documented with a Liability Release Form.

C. Discussion of Any Suspicious Behavior
Any inappropriate conduct or relationship between an adult volunteer worker and a member of the youth group or a child should be confronted immediately and reported to the associate pastor and investigated by the associate pastor or his designee.

(continued)

D. Windows in All Classroom Doors

E. Observe an Overnight Rule

All adult chaperones and supervisors should be cleared in advance with proper department directors.

F. Male Leaders and Children

Male leaders shall not be permitted to be alone for any reason with female children or youth. This includes rides to and from church and in an unsupervised situation on the church grounds and off the church property.

II. Reporting Procedures

An effective reporting procedure enhances the effort to protect children. Child molesters will not remain in a church where workers are trained to identify symptoms of child abuse and are encouraged to report suspicious behavior.

A. All suspicious behavior or observed incidents should be reported directly to the youth or children's pastor.

B. The youth or children's pastor will need to report the incident within twenty-four hours to the associate pastor for consultation.

C. State or local authorities will be contacted by the senior pastor or associate pastor before forty-eight hours, in verbal or written contact. A formal written report should be done for liability reasons.

D. All workers will, at the Covenant Renewal meeting, review training materials describing possible indicators and symptoms of child abuse.

E. All workers should report unhealthy symptoms (such as vomiting, open sores, bleeding). All reports should be documented in writing and brought immediately to the attention of the nursery or preschool coordinator.

F. Reporting procedures will be periodically taught to all workers and staff who work with minors at the Covenant Renewal meeting.

G. The church will check state child abuse reporting laws regularly because these laws are amended often.

CHILDREN'S MINISTRY APPLICATION

This ministry application will help serve all parishioners seeking a ministry opportunity for any position (volunteer or compensated) involving the supervision or custody of minors. Persons seeking to serve with children will be required to complete this form. It is being used to help Mount Paran Church of God provide a safe and secure environment for children who participate in our programs and use our facilities.

GENERAL

Last Name: _____ First Name: _____ Middle Initial: _____

Home #: _____ Work #: _____ Beeper # (if applicable): _____

Address: _____

City: _____ Zip: _____ Birth Date: __/__/__

Emergency Contact: _____ Phone #: _____

Spouse's Name: _____

List Children and Ages: _____

_____

Driver's License # and State: _____
(Please include a photocopy of your driver's license or other photo ID to confirm identity.)

Please check area of ministry interest.   Please check the time you are interested in serving.

❑ Nursery   ❑ Sunday 9:00 A.M.
❑ Preschool   ❑ Sunday 9:45 A.M.
❑ Grade School   ❑ Sunday 11:00 A.M.
                             ❑ Sunday 7:00 P.M.
                             ❑ Wednesday 7:00 P.M.

BACKGROUND

When did you join Mount Paran Church of God? _____

Have you previously served in a Mount Paran Central Ministry? ❑ Yes ❑ No

List other churches that you have attended regularly during the past five years:

_____

(continued)

List all previous church work (list each church's name and address, type of work performed, and dates):

_____

_____

_____

_____

_____

Have you been convicted or pleaded guilty to any crime? ❏ Yes ❏ No (If "Yes," please explain.)

TEMPERAMENT

Please circle the words below that best describe your temperament

Compassionate	Leader	Flexible	Intelligent	Introvert	Energetic
Communicator	Balanced	Feeler	Teachable	Extrovert	Self-starter
Prefer Routine	Laid-back	Thorough	Up Front	Strong-willed	Follower
Prefer Variety	Trusted	Honest	Sensitive	Risk-taker	Structured
Behind-the-Scenes	Humble	Reliable	Patient	Friendly	Loyal
Even-tempered	Work Alone	Team Player	Responsible	Thinker	

What are your areas of weakness?

REFERENCES

Please include one pastoral, one personal, and one professional reference.

Name: _____ Years Known: _____

Relationship: _____ Phone #: _____

Name: _____ Years Known: _____

Relationship: _____ Phone #: _____

Name: _____ Years Known: _____

Relationship: _____ Phone #: _____

(continued)

INTERVIEW

Please attach separate sheets of paper if more room is needed to answer the questions.

Do you feel called to serve in children's ministry? ❏ Yes ❏ No Why?

Why do you think it is important to work with children?

Have you ever been convicted of child abuse? ❏ Yes ❏ No (If "yes," please explain.)

Were you a victim of abuse or molestation while a minor? ❏ Yes ❏ No

If you prefer, you may refuse to answer this question, or you may discuss your answer in conference with the director of children's ministry rather than answering it in this form. Answering "Yes" or leaving it blank WILL NOT automatically disqualify an applicant for children's work.

EDUCATION

High School: _____ Did you graduate? ❏ Yes ❏ No

College: _____ Years? _____ Degree? _____

Other Schooling: _____

VOCATIONAL EXPERIENCE

What skills, natural talents, or special abilities do you possess?

(continued)

What employment/vocational experiences in the marketplace have you had that could be used in children's ministry?

GIFTS

Please check the top four gifts you feel you possess.

❏ Administration	❏ Communication	❏ Giving	❏ Intercession
❏ Teaching	❏ Discernment	❏ Healing	❏ Leadership
❏ Counseling	❏ Encouragement	❏ Helps	❏ Mercy
❏ Craftsmanship	❏ Evangelism	❏ Hospitality	❏ Prophecy
❏ Discipleship	❏ Other _____	❏ Other _____	❏ Other _____

TESTIMONY

Please give an account of your salvation experience and any other significant experiences with God.

REQUEST FOR CRIMINAL RECORDS CHECK AND AUTHORIZATION

Because we care about you and our kids, we now need to request your permission to perform a criminal records check. Please know that past mistakes will not necessarily negate you from ministry at the present time. However, in light of several recent court rulings, we now find it necessary to request your permission to obtain this information.

Your cooperation with this uncomfortable and awkward request is greatly appreciated.

I hereby request the _____ Police Department to release any information that pertains to any record of convictions contained in its files or in any criminal file maintained on me whether local, state, or national. I hereby release said police department from any and all liability resulting from such disclosure.

_____
Signature

_____
Print Name

_____
Print Maiden Name (if applicable)

_____
Print All Aliases

_____
Date of Birth

_____
Place of Birth

_____
Social Security Number

_____
Today's Date

Record Check Sent To:

Name: _____

Address: _____

_____

RECORD OF CONTACT WITH REFERENCE OR CHURCH
IDENTIFIED BY AN APPLICANT FOR YOUTH/CHILDREN OR ADULT WORK

CONFIDENTIAL

1. Name of Applicant: _____

2. Reference or church contact (if a church, identify both the church and person, or minister contacted):

   _____

3. Date and time of contact: _____

4. Person contacting the reference or church: _____

5. Method of contact (e.g., telephone, letter, personal conversation): _____

   _____

6. Summary of conversation (summarize the reference's or minister's remarks concerning the applicant's fitness and suitability for youth/children's/adult work):

   _____
   Legible Signature

   Position: _____

   Date: _____

(continued)

Chapter Seven

Tailored to Fit: A Flexibility Approach

**Park Chapel Christian Church
Greenfield, Indiana**

You've been worshiping at Park Chapel Christian Church for about three years and are enjoying your new church home. You're amazed, however, by all the "new folks" who have joined the congregation since your arrival. Park Chapel was running about 280 when you began attending; now it's over 550. You are aware that many children are present at Park Chapel. In fact, that's one of the reasons you joined. You wanted a caring community for your two children. So it didn't surprise you when the preschool coordinator asked about your interest and availability in working in the children's program.

What was surprising, however, was how understanding and accommodating the leadership was regarding your particular scheduling needs. Because you are a noncustodial parent, your weekend schedule is rather full. So you were delighted to learn that Park Chapel would flex with your needs, allowing deeper involvement but at a commitment level that was personally manageable. That's why you feel so at home in the Park Chapel family.

Telling us more about volunteerism at Park Chapel Christian Church is Mark Clark, their children's minister.

Step of Faith

+ + + + + + +

Park Chapel Christian Church in Greenfield, Indiana, is just over twelve years old, a daughter church of East 91st Street Christian Church in Indianapolis, Indiana. Park Chapel started with about fifty to sixty people. Within just a few Sundays, there were around one hundred. We had steady growth over the next six years. We started meeting in schools and have now been in our own building since 1994.

Three years ago, when the associate on staff was leaving, the elders decided to take a step of faith and hire not just one new person, but two. They hired me as the children's minister and Brian Lakin as the youth minister. I came in January 1996; Brian came in February. The congregation had been in their new building for only two years, but had already grown to an average attendance in the high two hundreds.

A Young Congregation

+ + + + + + +

We are a very young congregation. The average age of the membership is somewhere in the neighborhood of thirty-four. We have many large families, bringing us lots of children. We are in a dynamic time that averaged 23 percent growth for two years, then jumped to 40 percent growth.

This means that we continually need an expanding corps of volunteers. At the same time, we are also modifying our organizational structures. *We're finding it advantageous to departmentalize into tighter age groups.* That has allowed us to be much more specific in targeting the volunteers that we need. We don't just ask people to work in the children's area; we're more focused. When talking with a prospective worker, we let them know that we need "a person to work with two year olds the first hour, and another to work with first and second graders on Sunday nights."

Because we target specific ministry needs, we've had a much greater return than when we were generically asking for volunteers. When people didn't know exactly what they might be getting themselves into, they were not coming forward. But as we've become more focused, people say, "I can work with that age group. I'd be interested."

128

A lot of our helpers are discovered through relationships. Our teachers, helpers, and leaders are all on the lookout for new workers. But in addition to recruiting through relationships, *we have invited parents who benefit from our ministry to consider involvement in our programs*. If their children are in our program, we have positively communicated to them that they have gifts and abilities we would like to tap. It may be something as minor as taking care of the refreshments in a room or helping with a specific program. Effective ministry requires teams of willing workers.

Starting Without Pressure

✝ ✝ ✝ ✝ ✝ ✝ ✝

At Park Chapel, volunteers can begin their service in a limited capacity, which helps to take the pressure off of them. They know that their commitment is for one Sunday, for one hour or ninety minutes, depending upon what the need is. *It gives them an opportunity to test the waters* and see if a particular program is something that they'd desire for a longer term.

Due to our rapid growth, we have a lot of new families who are either formerly unchurched or are coming back to the church. For them, the idea of bringing their children and leaving them in a foreign environment is uncomfortable. They are watching to see how we treat the kids and take care of them. *So we have a standing invitation for parents to come into a classroom and be like wallpaper.* They can either be in their child's class or in another class. We want them to see what we do and how we do it, and to understand what we're trying to accomplish. We want to reassure them that their child is going to receive the best care we can possibly give. After observing class sessions, a number of these parents come back as helpers, assistants, and teachers.

Two other avenues that we use for recruitment are our *major outreach events:* Vacation Bible School and our Halloween alternative party. We recruit heavily for these events and volunteers usually come away feeling very good about their experiences. Volunteers are not surprised when a leader asks, "If you enjoyed Vacation Bible School, maybe you would enjoy doing this." And so we've found that Vacation Bible School not only serves as a strong outreach into our community, but also a strong inreach into our congregation.

When I came to Park Chapel, we put together a carnival that we called "Under the Big Top," which is now our Halloween alternative party. We took a circus theme and put some very creative people to work on it. We cleared out our auditorium, which is basically a gymnasium since we are in a Phase 1 building, and used all the floor space for booths and games. We set up a schedule and asked people to work either for the first hour or the second hour. Everyone was encouraged to bring families and friends. Family members could enjoy the whole evening, and the workers could join them for part of the evening. Each year, as a result of having an enjoyable time, several workers inquire, "Is there something else that I can do?"

Flexibility Encourages Participation

✝ ✝ ✝ ✝ ✝ ✝ ✝

Some teachers make a one-year commitment to serve a group of children each Sunday, short of death. We have others who volunteer on a permanent part-time basis. Some work on the first Sunday of each month; others one month out of every four. The schedules vary, but we have found that when we can be flexible, people are much more willing to participate.

When we become rigid, then we lose a lot of workers. We staff our programs with key people who will commit to every Sunday as a lead teacher. Then we surround them with a consistent group of workers who, as their schedules permit, will do some of the hands-on work with the kids. It helps everybody all the way around.

We also take a flexible approach to training. Summer has proven to be a great time for us to do more intensive teacher training than we are able to do at other times of the year. We offer daytime and evening training to accommodate working families, stay-at-home moms, and people working the swing shift.

Most of our training events are built into one hour-and-a-half session, but we'll schedule these events at four different times, varying them between weekdays, weekends, mornings, afternoons, and evenings. We try to make them available to as many people as possible.

If we're not flexible, we'll die. And that is the key. We want to find out what people's abilities and gifts are so that we can find a ministry fit for them. I learned early on in ministry that you may eventually make a square peg fit into a round hole, but neither the peg nor the hole will be happy about it. So I try not to coerce. I want people to come and enjoy what they're doing.

In order for someone to be a teacher or department team leader at Park Chapel, *they must be members in the congregation.* Obviously, those who communicate the faith must be in agreement with our biblical viewpoint. Furthermore, we want teachers who embrace our teaching philosophy. If they're going to be the main team communicating God's Word to our children, then we want to make sure we're all on the same page.

Teacher interviews are conducted by me or by one of our department leaders. Our department leaders are capable, trustworthy people. I personally interview everyone appointed to a lead teacher position. Our lead teachers have the latitude to recruit people as helpers, assistants, or substitutes. When someone is ready to move into a deeper level of service, I'm usually more active in that recruitment and interview.

Spare Tires for Jesus

In any ongoing ministry, emergency situations arise that require fill-in workers. *Substitute teachers are kind of like spare tires.* Most of us don't plan to use the little spare tire in the trunks of our cars, but when we're fifty miles from anywhere, we're glad they're there. At Park Chapel, we have some people who make great spare tires for Jesus. We don't use them on a week-in and week-out basis. But if I have to call them late Saturday night or even on Sunday and ask, "Can you teach the first and second graders today?" I know they can do it. Most of them are professional teachers. We use them as substitutes and trainers. Again, this gives us the flexibility to handle special situations.

We use middle schoolers and high schoolers as helpers, particularly during Vacation Bible School or other big events. On Sundays we allow teenagers to work in our children's areas on a consistent basis. One of our best teachers is a high school freshman. She is superb with two and three year olds. Many of our students are willing to help, and we're open to giving them service opportunities. We're trying to move all of our people beyond the point of being just receivers. We want them to be givers too.

Getting to Know You

+ + + + + + +

At Park Chapel, we have a monthly program called "Getting to Know Us and You." This casual social event provides an opportunity for visitors, new members, and whoever else is interested to meet with the ministry staff. It lasts around an hour-and-a-half, and we serve pie and coffee or other refreshments. We take about twenty minutes to present basic information about Park Chapel, our doctrinal positions, and a broad overview of each of our ministries. Then we say, "Okay, ask us questions."

This program has proven to be a great opportunity for meeting people. The sessions also open the door to service. We distribute *brochures about each of the ministry areas*, and hand them a copy of our latest *monthly newsletter.* I try to include an article about children's ministries in each edition. That publicity piece has even described the details of particular jobs, removing the mystery and fear of teaching for some volunteers.

We have *sign-up areas* in the Gathering Place, which is right outside our worship area. It's the central hub of our building. *Specific sign-up sheets list ministry opportunities.* A number of folks first learn about service possibilities at these sign-up areas.

For some people, particularly if they are coming out of an unchurched background, they don't know anything about our beliefs or programs, such as Sunday school or children's worship. Sometimes they are first exposed to service when a friend asks them to assist in a classroom situation. Even if they like what's going on, they may still have questions. Therefore, *we try to explain what we do in terms that anyone can understand*, for example, we call our helpers "room parents." Most people understand this concept. And as they grow in their faith and their desire to help, they begin to feel, "I can do that." It is at this point that we interview them and go into background checks as part and parcel of our service procedure.

Excellence, Not Extravagance

+ + + + + + +

With the rapid growth that we've experienced, *we try to keep the children's ministry as visible as possible.* People don't realize how many children we serve each week, so one Sunday we took all of our children and brought them before our adults during our worship services.

We did that with babes in arms and toddlers in wagons, on up to fifth graders carrying banners and signs. All of the children walked in a procession across the front of our auditorium. People had no idea that we had that many children in the building. As a result, they realize there is a need for help.

Something else we've done to improve visibility is to have specific names and logos for our various children's programs. God has blessed us with several members who are graphic artists, so we have tried to develop good-looking logo pieces to put into our church family's hands. If we put out a logo piece, we want it to be packaged well. We say, "Not extravagance, but excellence." We don't want it to be slick, but we do want people to recognize that somebody has spent time on this. If somebody invested time to do this right, this ministry must be important!

The logos are displayed in publicity pieces and on posters around our facilities. One of the logos we developed is for our children's worship. We call it "E-Town." When we say "E-Town," people respond with the question, "What does the E stand for?" The answer is "anything." We use it for energy or excitement or enthusiasm or exhortation. One of the men in the church has a theater background and has built backdrops that have the logo on them to use in the E-Town area. We try to use that logo whenever we can.

We also try to make our Sunday night program as identifiable as possible, for example, the first and second graders who meet on Sunday night are called Primary Believers. In their logo, the word "Believers" is very blocky and foundational looking. "Primary," which was designed in the three primary colors and was made to appear bright and cheery, sits right on top of "Believers." Another group is called "PC K.I.D.S." for Park Chapel kids. "PC" is big and splashy; "K.I.D.S." is more structured.

We also have "Time 4." This graphic is a clock face with the word "time" and the number four about where it would appear on the clock. "Time 4" prompts the question, "What's it time for?" Well, it's time for adventure, it's time for excitement, it's time for learning, it's time for worship, and it's time for camp. We can use it for a number of children's activities. The logo is easy to duplicate and use as a banner in ministry fairs, to mark rooms, and to announce meeting times.

One thing we're careful about when using a logo or stylized name is the need to attach a descriptor. If we say "Primary Believers," we always include that they are first and second graders. If the logo is "PC K.I.D.S.," we mention that that includes third through fifth graders. If it's "E-Town," we include that it is first through fourth grade worship. We try to operate from the perspective that not everyone who reads this has been to the church before or has seen a newsletter in the last six months. We try to give them the information they need to make a decision about their child's need or about coming into that area as a worker.

We have put the logos on paper, on the video monitor that scrolls announcements out in the Gathering Place, even on Bibles. We've put the logos at the top of a prayer list and asked people, "Will you be in prayer for these people who help your kids?" We've gotten some neat responses from that. We've also been able to develop a prayer team that is specifically oriented to the children's ministry.

Diverse Programs, Diverse Opportunities

✛ ✛ ✛ ✛ ✛ ✛ ✛

We have two services, one at 9:00 A.M. and the other at 10:30 A.M. During the first hour we have adult worship, and adult and children's Sunday school classes. During the second hour, we have adult worship and children's worship for first through fourth graders. For the younger ages, kindergarten on down, we have a Bible school-type program. During children's worship, we have the children for the full hour and ten minutes.

On Sunday evenings, we run a program for first through fifth graders. We've thought about weeknights but we run up against sports activities, Boy Scouts, and school activities. We've been able to protect Sunday night pretty well and meet early enough that we don't run into family time. Sunday evening activities are very different from our Sunday morning program. The work that volunteers do in this ministry is also different than Sunday mornings, so this allows us to draw additional people into service with Park's children.

Child Safety and Security

✛ ✛ ✛ ✛ ✛ ✛ ✛

We do not use a contract or have a commissioning service for our volunteers. But now that our church has grown from "everybody knows everybody" to "What's your name again?" we've made the shift into doing background checks. When a prospective worker wants to join a ministry team, *we conduct a background check* on that person. This principle has actually helped us. People see that we're taking the children's ministry seriously, and they want to be a part of that.

Child security begins when children first arrive and continues until they are picked up by the parent that dropped them off. In our nursery, for example, *we have developed a good check-in system for our children*. Philosophically, this goes hand in hand with background checks. Just as we make sure that we have accountability with our workers, we also make sure we have accountability with the parents.

Our Luke 2:52 Standard

✝ ✝ ✝ ✝ ✝ ✝

We have a *primary philosophy of ministry* in the children's area. It is based on Luke 2:52, which says, "Jesus grew in wisdom and stature, and in favor with God and man" (*New International Version*). *We use those four points to test ourselves in ministry*. If we're doing something in children's ministry, why are we doing it? Our programs should provide a solid time for a child to grow intellectually, to grow spiritually in his relationship with God, and to develop solid fellowship, all within a safe environment where we can take care of his physical needs. If an activity doesn't meet one of these purposes, we need to back up and ask, "Do we really need to do this? Is this a waste of energy, manpower, resources, or family time?

This philosophy is a great safeguard. Because we're growing rapidly, there are a lot of people who bring in ideas from different backgrounds. Even within our church, what may have worked well in one department does not necessarily work well in another. Our Luke 2:52 standard gives us the opportunity to hear what people are saying, then to pass their suggestions through this filter. People don't automatically feel slighted knowing that their suggestion was honestly considered, whether it was adopted or not. This has given our teachers tremendous freedom because they're no longer the bad guys when they don't use someone's suggestion.

When a concern or issue does arise, our teachers direct the person or problem to me. *Our teachers and department leaders know that I'm here to back them up*. I am their number one cheerleader, encourager, and supporter. If there's an accountability issue with them, then they also stand before me. Conversely, if I foul up, I have to raise my hand and say, "I failed. Thanks for reining me in." We have a high measure of accountability to each other.

I view my ministry as not just to children, but to their families and to our children's workers. I want to make sure they know that there is someone who loves them, prays for them, encourages and supports them, and wants the very best for them.

We want our volunteers to have an enjoyable experience. If someone has success, then they're usually willing to come back and do it again. They may be tired because they have dealt with troublesome two and three year olds who are going through separation anxiety. Or they may be dealing with parents who are going through separation anxiety. But we want them to feel that they have accomplished something good and have ministered to people that day.

Whether someone's ministry is changing lives or changing diapers, our people understand that there are no unimportant tasks. We use the analogy from Scripture that in the body of Christ, all of the parts are essential. Effective children's ministry requires lots and lots of "parts" in order to touch lives for Christ.

+ + + + + + +

All churches have problems—sometimes they are good problems. The 25 percent plus annual growth that Park Chapel Christian Church is experiencing is a good problem. Finding adequate space, parking, and finances are typical concerns. But in this vibrant, young congregation, no one faces a greater challenge than those responsible for staffing an effective children's ministry.

Like many churches, Park Chapel is doing many things right. A particular highlight is that this congregation is willing to utilize volunteers at a service level that is manageable within each individual's particular life situation. The word "flexibility" well describes Park's philosophy of inviting volunteers to minister. While the leadership is thrilled with and cultivates long-term commitments, they are also willing to flex with the kinds of pressing schedules that are all too common as we enter the new millennium.

Ministry Resources

The following materials are used at Park Chapel Christian Church in their Christian education ministries. Permission to use and adapt these resources in your congregation is granted. Duplication or distribution of these copyrighted materials for resale is prohibited.

Park Chapel Christian Church
1176 E. McKenzie
Greenfield, IN 46140
(317) 462-4513

> **These two pages make up a Children's Ministry Team brochure from Park Chapel.**

Dear Family,

The Children's Ministry Team of Park Chapel wants to minister to your children. We offer a well-balanced program that is tailored for each age group. We provide a secure atmosphere for infants, creative classes for toddlers, and a stimulating learning environment for youngsters through the fifth grade. We look forward to the opportunity of teaching your children in an enjoyable learning experience.

> Sincerely,
> The leaders, teachers, helpers, and support staff of the Children's Ministry Team

For more information, contact the Children's Ministry Team at
> Park Chapel Christian Church
> Office: 462-4513
> Fax: 462-6850
> E-mail: parkchapel@aol.com

Our Mission
Based on Luke 2:52

The mission of the Children's Ministry Team is to lead children to a relationship with Christ by helping them to grow in:

> **Wisdom**—by providing opportunities for learning and applying God's Word to their lives.
> **Stature**—by providing opportunities for physical activities and fun in the safest environment possible.
> **Favor With God**—by providing opportunities to develop a meaningful knowledge of God through prayer, study, and thought.
> **Favor With Man**—by providing opportunities for social interaction with other children their age.

The mission cannot be accomplished without dedicated men and women who love God and are willing to care for His children. WILL YOU PRAYERFULLY CONSIDER HOW YOU CAN SERVE IN CHILDREN'S MINISTRIES?

(continued)

Early Childhood

A Nursery is available for babies and toddlers during each worship service. Children are cared for in a safe, sanitized, and secure environment. This allows the children to be cared for in a loving atmosphere while their parents enjoy a distraction-free worship and learning atmosphere.

Bible School Classes are offered for children ages two through kindergarten during the Sunday morning services. Active learning, storytelling, and fun songs are just part of how our loving workers share Jesus and the Bible with children.

The Baby Recognition Service takes place at the beginning of the second worship service on Mother's Day. At this service, we introduce all of the children born in the last year and their parents to the congregation. There is a special time for prayer for the children and parents and the presentation of a small gift. Please contact the church office if you would like to participate.

Elementary

Bible School Classes are offered for first through fifth graders during the Sunday Bible school time. Our teachers use a wide variety of age-appropriate methods, materials, activities, and curriculums to communicate God's Word to the children. Particular emphasis is given toward life application.

E-Town is the children's worship time. It is a celebration time of music, prayer, listening, learning, and laughing. The messages are a series of visualized parables presented by the "E-Team," a dedicated group of adults acting out childhood situations.

"Go for the Gold" is the theme for the Primary Believers (first and second graders) and PC K.I.D.S. (third through fifth graders). These groups meet the first and third Sunday nights of the month. These are activity-oriented learning times with incentive-based goals for service, attendance, and memorization. Both groups also provide fun trips and outings.

Special Events & Activities

Vacation Bible School is an important part of our summer ministry to children. It is a fun learning event for all four year olds through fifth graders. We use an activity-oriented program that encourages each child to participate. Lively music, games, crafts, videos, snacks (made by the kids), and unique teaching times mark this week.

Halloween Alternative Party. In a day and age when occult influences are rising and the public safety of children is a concern to all parents, this event is offered as a joyful alternative to the traditional celebration of Halloween. It is a carnival-type evening with games for all ages and skill levels. Appropriate costuming is welcome and each family is asked to contribute one bag of candy.

Children's Choir. The children's music program is off to a great start with the presentation of "Super Gift From Heaven" and "As the Flag Goes By." Check the church newsletter and bulletin for future rehearsal times and dates.

This is a sample bookmarker used at Park Chapel.

I WILL PRAY FOR:

Elders
Roger Hattem
Jim Schildmier
Mike Sears
Richard Woolard

Ministers
Mark Clark
Brian Larkin
David Woods

PC K.I.D.S. Leaders
Becky Hall
Carole Miller

Bible School Teachers
Clyde & Laura Diewert
Jim & Twyla Schildmier

E-Town
Ginay Bowman
Mike & Cathy Canny
Mark & Deborah Clark
Mike & Jamie Jann
Julianna Lewis
Shirley Matlock
Susan Ness
Trisha Rutledge
Dana Schmitt
Chris Weber
Kurt Woosley

The Praise Co.
Linda Cherry
Susan Ness

Pumpkin Patch Party!
October 31, 6:30 P.M.–8:30 P.M.

Yeeeeeeeeeah! It's time to get out your country finery. We are gonna have us a party in the Pumpkin Patch! All boys and girls are invited to come and share in the fun!

The theme is a country fair with games for all ages and skill levels, storytellers, refreshments, clowns, face painting, and more. Come dressed as a farmer, cowboy/girl, produce, livestock, etc. Be creative! Other costumes will be welcome as long as they are appropriate for the evening. Devils, ghosts, witches, monsters, and other seemingly evil or violent characters are inappropriate and will not be welcome.

Admission is one factory-sealed bag of individually wrapped candies per family.

In a day and age when occultic influences are on the rise and the public safety of children must be taken seriously, the children's ministry of Park Chapel wishes to provide a joyful alternative to the traditional celebration of Halloween.

Pumpkin Patch Party Workers Needed!

Will you be a partner with the children's ministry in this event? We need workers to staff the game booths, help with setup and cleanup, assist with food, serve as greeters at the door, help secure small prizes as giveaways (promotional items, "french fry cards," pencils, etc.), and to pray for the impact of this event.

Sign-up sheets will be in the Sunday bulletin and also at a table in the Gathering Place.

Primary Believers/PC K.I.D.S. Off to a Great Start!

Our fall program got off to a terrific start with **90 1st through 5th graders** there to make sure of it! Thanks to the **40 adults and teens** who staffed the games, prepared the food, handled registrations, and made it all work.

Unsung Heroes

There is a group of people it is very easy to forget about unless they are not there. They are the **children's workers**. Each Sunday, these men, women, and teens provide quality teaching and care for the children placed in their charge. From **nursery to 5th graders** during Bible School and worship, they diligently strive to communicate God's love through lessons, crafts, songs, drama, activities, and more. **Parents**, take a few moments over the next few weeks to stop and let them know how much you **appreciate their efforts**. Not only do your children receive first-class care, but these workers provide the freedom you and others need to learn and worship without distractions.

Primary Believers/ PC K.I.D.S.
Schedules/Medical Release Forms

Make sure to pick up a fall schedule of the meetings and outings. You will find them on the Info Tower in the Gathering Place along with the medical release forms. **Parents, please complete and turn in a medical form for your child/ children**. We must have a current form on file for your children to go on our outings.

Special thanks to **Becky Hall**, **Pam Sever**, and **Joyce West** for coordinating and recruiting the workers, to the Fraternal Order of Police for the use of the dunking tank, and to the Greenfield Fire Department for filling the tank.

These are logos used at Park Chapel.

Ministry Resources Listing

✝ ✝ ✝ ✝ ✝ ✝ ✝